FREE VIDEO

Essential Test Tips Video from Trivium Test Prep!

Thank you for purchasing from Trivium Test Prep!
We're honored to help you prepare for your exam.
To show our appreciation, we're offering a

FREE *Essential Test Tips* Video

Our video includes 35 test preparation strategies that will make you successful on your big exam. All we ask is that you email us your feedback and describe your experience with our product. Amazing, awful, or just so-so: we want to hear what you have to say!

> To receive your **FREE *Essential Test Tips* Video**, please email us at
> **5star@triviumtestprep.com.**

Include "Free 5 Star" in the subject line and the following information in your email:

1. The title of the product you purchased.
2. Your rating from 1 – 5 (with 5 being the best).
3. Your feedback about the product, including how our materials helped you meet your goals and ways in which we can improve our products.
4. Your full name and shipping address so we can send your **FREE *Essential Test Tips* Video**.

If you have any questions or concerns please feel free to contact us directly at:
5star@triviumtestprep.com.

Thank you!

– Trivium Test Prep Team

SHRM CP Exam Prep 2023-2024:

450+ Practice Questions and
SHRM Study Guide [3rd Edition]

Elissa Simon

Copyright ©2023 by Trivium Test Prep

ISBN-13: 9781637983928

ALL RIGHTS RESERVED. By purchase of this book, you have been licensed one copy for personal use only. No part of this work may be reproduced, redistributed, or used in any form or by any means without prior written permission of the publisher and copyright owner. Trivium Test Prep; Accepted, Inc.; Cirrus Test Prep; and Ascencia Test Prep are all imprints of Trivium Test Prep, LLC.

SHRM was not involved in the creation or production of this product, is not in any way affiliated with Trivium Test Prep, and does not sponsor or endorse this product. All test names (and their acronyms) are trademarks of their respective owners. This study guide is for general information and does not claim endorsement by any third party.

Image(s) used under license from Shutterstock.com

Table of Contents

Online Resources vii

Introduction ix

1 Business Strategy and Ethics 1

The Role of Human Resource Management in the Organization 1
Business Acumen 5
The Strategic Planning Process 12
Navigating the Organization 17
Organizational Design and Development 19
Organizational Change and Growth 22
Mergers and Acquisitions 24
Ethics 26
Answer Key 29

2 Leading and Communicating in the Workplace 31

Leadership 31
Relationship Management 35
Communication 39
Global and Cultural Effectiveness 42
Answer Key 46

3 Workforce Planning and Management 47

Equal Employment Opportunity 47
Affirmative Action Planning 54
Job Descriptions 56
Staff Planning and the Recruitment Process 58
Managing the Workforce 61
Succession Planning 62
Immigration in the Workplace 64
Answer Key 66

4 Total Rewards: Compensation and Benefits 67

What Are Total Rewards? 67
Compensation 68
Payroll 76
Severance Pay 78
Benefits 78
Work-Life Balance Programs 85
Recognition Programs 85
Professional Development Programs 86
Answer Key 88

5 Employee and Labor Relations 89

Labor Relations 89
Federal Labor Law 94
Company Policies and Culture 98
Dispute Resolution 101
Employee Discipline and Terminations 104
Global Employee Relations 106

v

Answer Key 108

6 Learning, Development, and Evaluation — 109

Training and Learning 109
Employee Feedback and
Performance Appraisals 115
Critical Evaluation 117
Answer Key 122

7 Risk Management — 123

Legal Compliance 123
Safety and Health 125
Business Continuity 129
Privacy and Confidentiality 131

Corporate Social Responsibility 134
Answer Key 136

8 SHRM Practice Test — 137

Knowledge-Based Questions 137
Situational Judgment Questions 147
Knowledge-Based Answer Key 159
Situational Judgment Answer Key 164

Online Resources

Trivium Test Prep includes online resources with the purchase of this study guide to help you fully prepare for your SHRM exam.

Practice Test

In addition to the practice test included in this book, we also offer an online exam. Since many exams today are computer based, practicing your test-taking skills on the computer is a great way to prepare.

Review Questions

Need more practice? Our review questions use a variety of formats to help you memorize key terms and concepts.

Flash Cards

Trivium Test Prep's flash cards allow you to review important terms easily on your computer or smartphone.

Cheat Sheets

Review the core skills you need to master the exam with easy-to-read Cheat Sheets.

From Stress to Success

Watch "From Stress to Success," a brief but insightful YouTube video that offers the tips, tricks, and secrets experts use to score higher on the exam.

Reviews

Leave a review, send us helpful feedback, or sign up for Trivium Test Prep promotions—including free books!

Access these materials at:

www.triviumtestprep.com/shrm-online-resources

Introduction

Congratulations on choosing to take the SHRM Certified Professional (SHRM-CP) exam! By purchasing this book, you've taken an important step on your human resources (HR) career path.

This guide will provide you with a detailed overview of the SHRM-CP, so you will know exactly what to expect on exam day. We'll take you through all of the concepts covered on the exam and give you the opportunity to test your knowledge with practice questions. Even if it's been a while since you last took a major exam, don't worry; we'll make sure you're more than ready!

What is the SHRM-CP?

The Society for Human Resource Management (SHRM) offers the SHRM-CP (SHRM-Certified Professional) exam to accredit human resources professionals. Candidates who pass the SHRM-CP can demonstrate that they have mastered certain core HR competencies.

The Society for Human Resource Management (SHRM)

The Society for Human Resource Management (SHRM) is a US-based organization with a global reach. It has over three hundred thousand members worldwide comprising HR professionals and executives. Its goals are to support the profession of human resources and advance HR practices. For more information on the SHRM and to become a member, please visit www.shrm.org.

SHRM-CP Certification

Why get SHRM-CP certification? First, it shows your knowledge and expertise in HR. In fact, candidates may not even apply for the exam without meeting certain requirements (see below). Successful candidates will have passed a test that addresses the main competencies and issues in human resources today. Having your certification will allow you to pursue more advanced job opportunities and negotiate a higher salary. It also shows your commitment to the profession and to improving your own knowledge and understanding.

What's on the SHRM-CP?

There are 160 questions on the SHRM-CP exam. Ninety-five questions are knowledge based and test your subject-matter proficiency. Sixty-five questions are situational judgment items (SJIs). On SJIs, you will read a summary of a short, realistic HR scenario and answer related questions.

Of the 134 questions, twenty-four are field test items, meaning they are used for research and do not count towards your score. However, you will not know which questions are unscored, so be sure to answer every question.

All questions are multiple-choice. The exam is computer-based, and applicants have four hours to complete it.

The material on the SHRM-CP exam is based on the **SHRM Body of Applied Skills and Knowledge (BASK).** The BASK contains three Behavioral Competency Clusters: Leadership, Interpersonal, and Business. It also has three Knowledge Domains: People, Organization, and Workplace. All questions on the SHRM-CP exam will fall under one of these categories.

What's on the SHRM-CP?	
BEHAVIORAL COMPETENCY CLUSTERS	
Leadership	17% of exam
Business	16.5% of exam
Interpersonal	16.5% of exam
HR KNOWLEDGE DOMAINS	
People	18% of exam
Organization	18% of exam
Workplace	14% of exam
Total:	**4 hours for 134 questions**

Questions will not be labeled by type, but it is helpful to have an overview of the content they will cover.

Behavioral Competencies

The three Behavioral Competency Clusters—**Leadership, Business,** and **Interpersonal**—comprise a percentage of questions on the SHRM-CP exam.

The SHRM recognizes Behavioral Competencies subsumed under the Behavioral Competency Clusters.

Behavioral Competencies	
Leadership	• Leadership and Navigation • Ethical Practice • Diversity, Equity, and Inclusion
Interpersonal	• Relationship Management • Communication • Global Mindset
Business	• Business Acumen • Consultation • Analytical Aptitude

The Leadership cluster includes three Behavioral Competencies: Leadership and Navigation; Ethical Practice; and Diversity, Equity, and Inclusion. **Leadership and Navigation** questions address the ability of a candidate to effectively strategize. Questions may be about directing organizational change, understanding and creating an organizational mission, and implementing HR initiatives. **Ethical Practice** questions address situations where an HR professional needs to exhibit integrity. Questions may concern accountability or how an HR professional promotes an organization's core values. **Diversity, Equity, and Inclusion (DEI)** questions concern how HR can support DEI in the workplace, ensuring all individuals are treated with respect and fairness.

The Interpersonal cluster encompasses three Behavioral Competencies: Relationship Management, Communication, and Global and Cultural Effectiveness. **Relationship Management** questions focus on professional networking, teamwork, and conflict management and resolution. **Communication** questions address the delivery of information throughout the organization to diverse stakeholders, including best practices for transmitting messages. They also ask about listening and interpreting information received from others. **Global Mindset** questions test an examinee's knowledge of considering all perspectives in the workplace, ability to practice HR with a global mindset, and understanding of how to promote diversity in the workplace.

Finally, the Business cluster includes three Behavioral Competencies: Business Acumen, Consultation, and Critical Evaluation. **Business Acumen** questions involve understanding an organization's general operations and functions. Questions may discuss using business tools to conduct HR analyses and how an HR professional can support an organization's overall functioning. **Consultation** questions address business challenges and winning support for HR to meet business needs. **Analytical Aptitude** questions concern the analysis and interpretation of relevant data and information for HR initiatives.

HR Knowledge Domains

The HR Knowledge Domains reflect overall HR knowledge, or the technical competency of HR expertise. There are three Knowledge Domains: **People**, **Organization**, and **Workplace**. These domains are further subdivided into fourteen HR Functional Areas.

The Knowledge Domains and Functional Areas	
People	HR Strategy
	Talent Acquisition
	Employee Engagement and Retention
	Learning and Development
	Total Rewards
Organization	Structure of the HR Function
	Organizational Effectiveness and Development
	Workforce Management
	Employee and Labor Relations
	Technology Management
Workplace	Managing a Global Workforce
	Risk Management
	Corporate Social Responsibility
	US Employment Law and Regulations

The Knowledge Domain of People includes five HR Functional Areas: HR Strategic Planning, Talent Acquisition, Employee Engagement and Retention, Learning and Development, and Total Rewards. **HR Strategy** questions address how to build, implement, and manage HR strategies that will support an organization's success. **Talent Acquisition** questions ask about how to develop an organization's workforce—the hiring process. Questions about **Employee Engagement and Retention** concern how to keep that workforce: improving relationships between talent and the organization, communicating expectations for employees, and supporting personnel. **Learning and Development** questions ask about HR's role in developing employees' competency to advance the needs of an organization. Finally, **Total Rewards** questions address compensation and benefits.

The Knowledge Domain of Organization also includes five HR Functional Areas: Structure of the HR Function, Organizational Effectiveness and Development, Workforce Management, Employee and Labor Relations, and Technology Management. Questions on the **Structure of the HR Function** address organization within the HR department itself. **Organizational Effectiveness and Development** questions test a candidate's knowledge of an organization more generally, beyond just the HR department, as well as the need for organizational change and restructuring. **Workforce Management** questions concern issues like workforce planning, succession planning, and how to fill gaps in talent. **Employee and Labor Relations** questions engage in the details of employee and labor policy, such as conditions of employment. Finally, **Technology Management** questions ask about how technology can support HR, technological tools, and general policies about the use of technology in the workplace.

The Knowledge Domain of Workplace includes four HR Functional Areas: Managing a Global Workforce, Risk Management, Corporate Social Responsibility, and US Employment Law and Regulations. **Managing a Global Workforce** questions address the management of global workforces. **Risk Management** questions test your knowledge of risk assessment and how to minimize risk. **Corporate Social Responsibility** questions ask how an organization can promote philanthropic and ethical activities both within the organization and in the greater community. Finally, **US Employment Law and Regulations** questions test your knowledge of legal issues related to employing talent in the United States.

How is the SHRM-CP Scored and Administered?

Eligibility Requirements

You must meet certain requirements to take the SHRM-CP—a combination of professional and educational experience.

Candidates with an HR-related bachelor's degree must have one year of professional experience in an HR role. Those candidates who have a bachelor's degree in another specialty must have at least two years of experience working in HR before they can take the SHRM-CP.

Candidates with HR-related graduate degrees must currently be working in an HR role. Candidates with other graduate degrees may only take the SHRM-CP after they have worked for one year in human resources.

Some applicants are eligible with less than a bachelor's degree, assuming they have HR experience. Candidates who have not completed their bachelor's degree must have at least four years of experience in an HR role before they can take the test. Candidates who are working toward their bachelor's degree in HR must have three years of experience in HR and be working in HR at the time of the test.

Applying for the Exam

The SHRM-CP is offered twice yearly—in the spring and in the winter. A candidate who meets the eligibility requirements may apply to the SHRM to take the SHRM-CP exam. To apply for the exam, an account must be created at www.shrmcertification.org. All interested candidates must complete an application form. Applicants who require testing accommodations may fill out the forms for those accommodations at this time.

Registration fees vary depending on when they are paid and membership status of the applicant. Check with SHRM for the most current details.

The SHRM-CP is administered by computer at Prometric testing centers around the nation. As of 2022, it may also be taken remotely. Plan to arrive at least **thirty minutes before the exam** to complete biometric screening. Bring at least one form of **government-issued photo ID** and be prepared to be photographed and have your fingertips scanned. You will also be scanned with a metal detector wand before entering the test room. Your primary ID must be unexpired, government issued, include a recent photograph and signature, and match the name under which you registered to take the test. If you do not have proper ID, you will not be allowed to take the test.

You will not be allowed to bring any personal items into the testing room, such as calculators or phones. You may not bring pens, pencils, or scratch paper. Other prohibited items include hats, scarves, and coats. You may, however, wear religious garments. Prometric provides lockers for valuables; you can keep your ID and locker key with you.

To maintain certification, you must earn at least sixty professional development credits or take the exam again. Recertification is required every three years. Please see www.shrmcertification.org for more details.

Scoring

The number of questions you answer correctly will be added up to obtain your raw score. Your raw score is then scaled. Scaled scores range from 120 – 200. A passing score is 200. This, however, doesn't mean you must answer every single question correctly to pass; it means that the scale only goes up to 200.

Whether they pass or not, all examinees will receive feedback about their score on a document called the *score report*. The **score report** includes both an examinee's score and information about the test taker's competency in the SHRM Knowledge Domains and Behavioral Competency Clusters. A chart will indicate a candidate's areas of strength as well as areas for improvement. This feedback is helpful for all candidates: it allows them to discover areas for improvement and pursue appropriate professional development. Again, examinees may still pass the exam and earn their SHRM-CP even if they answered some questions incorrectly.

About This Guide

This guide will help you master the most important test topics and develop critical test-taking skills. We have built features into our books to prepare you for your exam and increase your score.

Along with a detailed summary of the test's format, content, and scoring, we offer an in-depth overview of the content knowledge required to pass the test. Throughout the guide, you'll find sidebars that provide interesting information, highlight key concepts, and review content so that you can solidify your understanding. You can also test your knowledge with sample questions throughout the text as well as practice questions. We're pleased you've chosen Trivium to be a part of your journey!

1 Business Strategy and Ethics

The Role of Human Resource Management in the Organization

Human resource management describes the activities essential to managing an organization's employees, or its human capital. HR professionals oversee compensation and benefits, training and development, recruitment and hiring, strategic management, and other functions.

HR departments recruit, retain, and motivate the best employees for the organization. To do so, they must keep the company competitive in terms of compensation, benefits, learning opportunities, career advancement, work-life balance, and other matters important to employees.

At the same time, HR plays an important business role in the organization. HR management strategizes how to allocate staff appropriately, maintain regulatory compliance, and prevent risks. Aligning "people needs" with business needs is essential to the organization's viability and attractiveness in the marketplace.

HR functions or areas of expertise include recruitment, health and safety, employee relations, compensation and benefits, and compliance. HR practitioners may perform a combination of these or specialize in one or a few. Small businesses that do not have a dedicated HR professional will sometimes outsource these functions or join a professional employer organization to get the same benefits of an internal HR team.

Recruitment

Talent acquisition or **recruitment** by a human resources organization can be performed through internal recruiters, employment specialists, or HR generalists. As part of the overall recruitment process, these professionals advertise and post jobs, source resumes, screen candidates, conduct first-round interviews, and coordinate with the hiring manager (or team).

In many organizations, recruiters' success is measured by the time taken to fill job openings (requisitions) and the number of positions filled. Recruitment can also be performed by external agencies or headhunters.

Health and Safety

Workplace **health and safety** is essential, especially in industries in which workers operate heavy machinery, are exposed to chemicals or harmful substances, or work in otherwise dangerous places or situations. Employee safety is mandated through the federal **Occupational Safety and Health Act of 1970**. HR often facilitates or oversees health and safety training and maintains federally mandated logs for workplace injuries and fatalities that must be reported to the government. HR also manages workers' compensation issues for on-the-job injuries.

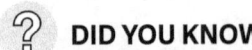

DID YOU KNOW?

Employers generally must keep a record of on-the-job illnesses, accidents, and injuries for up to five years. And, they must keep any medical records of these injuries or illnesses for thirty years.

Employee Relations

Employee relations strengthen the employer-employee relationship through measuring job satisfaction, maintaining employee engagement, and resolving workplace conflicts or grievances. Employee relations also include coaching employees and managers to handle difficult situations, investigating sexual harassment and discrimination claims, placing employees on performance improvement plans, and terminating employees.

In a unionized work environment, labor relations functions may include negotiating collective bargaining agreements, facilitating the grievance process, and interpreting union contracts. The employee and labor relations functions of HR may be combined and handled by one specialist, or they might be entirely separate functions managed by two HR specialists with expertise in each area.

Compliance

Compliance with local, state, and federal labor laws is an essential HR function. Noncompliance can result in litigation and governmental complaints of unfair employment practices and unsafe working conditions, fines from the government, and overall dissatisfaction among employees. HR staff must be aware of federal, state, and local employment laws such as the Fair Labor Standards Act, Title VII of the Civil Rights Act, the National Labor Relations Act, the Family and Medical Leave Act, and many more. To comply with these laws and maintain fairness in the organization, HR professionals help develop company policies and procedure manuals.

Compensation and Benefits

Like employee and labor relations, the **compensation and benefits** functions of HR are often handled by one HR specialist with dual expertise. HR functions include setting compensation and evaluating competitive pay practices. A compensation and benefits specialist may also negotiate group health coverage rates with insurers and coordinate with the retirement savings fund administrator. Payroll might be conducted by the compensation and benefits section of HR, but in many cases it is handled by the finance department or outsourced to an external provider.

Training and Development

Employers must provide employees with the **training** and tools necessary for their success. New employees should go through an orientation to help them transition to the new organization as part of the onboarding process and undergo adequate training for their job. Many HR departments also coordinate leadership training and ongoing professional development activities. Depending on the organization's financial resources, programs such as tuition assistance programs for college or advanced degrees may be offered as part of training and development.

HR Generalist and HR Specialist: What Is the Difference?

HR professionals typically fall into one of two categories: generalist or specialist. **HR generalists**, also called HR managers or **HR business partners**, have a broad range of responsibilities in one or more of the functional areas of human resources. Larger organizations usually have **HR specialists** with technical knowledge and skills in specific areas.

There are different levels of generalists and specialists in an organization, depending on its size, budget, and other needs. Examples of specialist job titles are listed in the table below.

TABLE 1.1. Functional Areas of HR and Related Job Titles	
FUNCTIONAL AREA	**JOB TITLE EXAMPLES**
Recruiting	<ul><li>Recruiter</li><li>Recruiting Assistant or Recruiting Coordinator</li><li>Talent Acquisition Specialist</li><li>Staffing Manager</li></ul>
Training and Organizational Development	<ul><li>Learning and Organizational Development Manager</li><li>Organizational Development Specialist</li></ul>
Compensation and Benefits	<ul><li>Compensation Analyst</li><li>Benefits Specialist</li><li>Total Rewards Manager</li></ul>
Employee and Labor Relations	<ul><li>Performance Manager Specialist</li><li>Employee Relations Manager</li><li>Labor Relations Manager</li></ul>
Safety	<ul><li>Risk Management Specialist</li><li>Workers' Compensation Specialist</li></ul>
HR Information Systems	<ul><li>HRIS Administrator</li><li>HRIS Manager</li></ul>

Policies and Procedures

As organizations grow, they must develop policies and procedures to maintain consistency throughout the organization, convey important information to employees, and comply with federal and state laws. Clear, well-communicated **human resources policies and procedures** ensure consistent messages and administration throughout the organization. Documented policies can also protect the organization in case of lawsuits or complaints. Finally, HR policies and procedures help the organization formalize its approach to achieving compliance with federal law.

Policies should support managers in handling personnel issues. A supervisor who reads and understands the written policies of the organization can answer employee questions, respond to complaints, and handle minor disciplinary issues without always involving the human resources department. For example, if two employees in different departments are consistently late or are not meeting performance standards, having established policies in place will help managers treat employees fairly. If an employee questions how the supervisor handles an employment issue, the supervisor can reference the HR policies, helping the supervisor maintain authority while remaining unbiased.

Policies and procedures help employees too. By providing **handbooks** to employees, organizations empower them with information, helping them better understand their own responsibilities. Employees with questions about work hours, paychecks, dress code, paid time off, harassment, or other issues can find answers on their own. In addition, complete policies provide employees with guidance on whom to contact with concerns about their employment or other issues. Handbooks should be reviewed carefully and updated regularly because they may create an enforceable contract.

Finally, the manual is an example of how the organization administers policies consistently and fairly. In the event of litigation or a complaint about an employment action, policies protect the organization. Human resource professionals should reference the policies when responding to questions and coach supervisors on the appropriate methods or procedures to document employee disciplinary problems. Policies and procedures should be reviewed periodically and updated to reflect changes in federal and state laws relating to employees, as well as changes in the work environment or organizational structure.

EXAMPLES

1. A practitioner with expertise in a specific area of human resources is called:
    - **A)** HR generalist
    - **B)** HR manager
    - **C)** HR specialist
    - **D)** HR expert

2. The primary reason employee handbooks should be reviewed carefully and continually updated is because they may

   A) be available to the public for review.
   B) create an enforceable contract.
   C) provide new employees with important information.
   D) be the only way the employer communicates with employees.

Business Acumen

Business acumen means speaking the language of business, understanding the multiple functions of an organization, and being able to show the value of HR to the organization. In recent years, the tactical HR generalist role has changed into a business partnership with senior leadership to develop and execute personnel strategies. Still, the administrative and tactical aspects of HR remain necessary for business operations. To be influential, HR business partners must position themselves as tactical operators, strategic advisors, and champions for change.

Developing a strong understanding of the organization, its operations, and its external environment is essential for any HR business partner to become a strategic advisor to senior management. HR business partners must align themselves closely with the values of the organization and the vision of its leaders in order to be seen as valuable partners. To do this they must:

- develop in-depth knowledge about the business, including its operations, financials, and strategy
- build key relationships in the organization to influence the strategic agenda
- earn leaders' trust so HR can contribute to business results
- prioritize processes that deliver the most benefits
- develop credibility through competence, honesty, and high standards
- champion HR solutions that add to the bottom line today and for future needs
- act as a catalyst for continued business performance

As business partners, HR practitioners share the responsibility for the business's success by executing HR strategies that lead to tangible results. HR partners quantify HR's contribution to business performance and staff effectiveness in all operations. HR business partners ensure that duties are assigned to those with appropriate qualifications, design meaningful career paths to motivate employees, actively manage talent, create staffing and succession plans, and foster an open work environment where ideas are shared.

What Is Strategic Management?

Over the past century, companies have grown larger and more complicated as the demands of consumers and the business environment have grown more complex and nuanced. Products are now created using elaborate processes with multiple workers and machines. Additionally, as the US economy has evolved from primarily manufacturing products to providing services, companies must accommodate demand and trends to stay competitive. Over time, companies have developed new processes, restructured their personnel, adopted new tools, and reevaluated management practices to ensure that their employees are able to achieve these overarching goals.

To stay competitive in a continually evolving global marketplace, business leaders must be able to quickly respond and adapt to change in the industry, economy, workforce, and regulatory environment. They must know their clients' needs and develop useful products and services to meet those needs. Successful business leaders continually scan the environment, make predictions, and develop business plans to stay competitive. This ongoing process of creation, research, reassessment, and development is called **strategic management**. Strategic management is important to human resources professionals because it affects how HR adds value to the organization through policies, procedures, and programs.

Strategic HR management, then, is achieved when HR leaders and practitioners develop overall management strategies for the company. Since organizations are composed of people, the human resources function must focus on those items that impact the people side of the organization. When the organization must respond to changes in the marketplace, industry, or regulatory environment, HR practitioners are responsible for aligning the organization's people, policies, and processes with these changes. To be successful, they must collaborate with business leadership to stay aware of business goals, objectives, and strategic vision.

Strategic Alignment

HR is not only a business partner; it is also a strategic partner to the organization. HR must align the strategic initiatives of the HR function with those of the organization. In **strategic alignment**, HR balances the strategies of the business with the needs of employees and the requirements of laws and legislation. More than ever, organizational culture and employee morale are strategically important to the success of the business.

Strategic alignment from the HR perspective incorporates five critical components:

- workforce planning
- organizational capability assessment
- organizational development and structure
- diversity and inclusion
- change management

HR is no longer seen as the personnel department processing paperwork. Rather, HR is a part of the organization's broader decision-making process. Areas like employee compensation, talent acquisition, training and development, and organizational design must support the direction and mission of the business as a whole. To make decisions, HR uses **analytics** and **business intelligence** tools. Some of these tools will be discussed in detail below.

HR also plays a critical role in achieving key organizational initiatives by leading organizational design and change management programs. HR formulates, implements, and monitors the people side of the business by using analytics to measure the success and **return on investment (ROI)** of programs and initiatives. The leadership looks to HR for the systems and processes that will ensure the strategic HR goals and metrics are met and will support the organization as it works toward its mission and vision.

Business and Competitive Awareness

As a business partner, HR must learn and understand the organization's business operations, functions, products, and services. It is not enough that HR understands only the HR function and the laws and rules that surround it. To be a strategic partner, HR must understand the core business of the organization and the forces that impact this function.

Regularly monitoring and responding to the **external environment** is critical to the organization's success. HR must remain keenly aware of changes in the external environment and respond strategically by implementing HR solutions. **External forces** include the economy, consumer demand, laws and regulations, technology, and the labor force. Being proactive and adapting to these changes keeps an organization strong.

HR professionals use many tools to assess and analyze such forces. The **PESTLE analysis** allows HR professionals to conduct situational analysis before implementing a strategy or plan. The PESTLE analysis shows how external factors may impact an organization.

- **P**olitical factors include government stability, policies, foreign relations, taxes, etc.
- **E**conomic factors include inflation, interest rates, unemployment, trade, and other issues.
- **S**ocial factors include culture, age distribution, public health, population growth, and so on.
- **T**echnological factors include innovation, automation, awareness of and access to technology.
- **L**egal factors include consumer protection laws, antitrust laws, copyright laws, and other laws.
- **E**nvironmental factors include climate change, weather events, and risk of natural disasters.

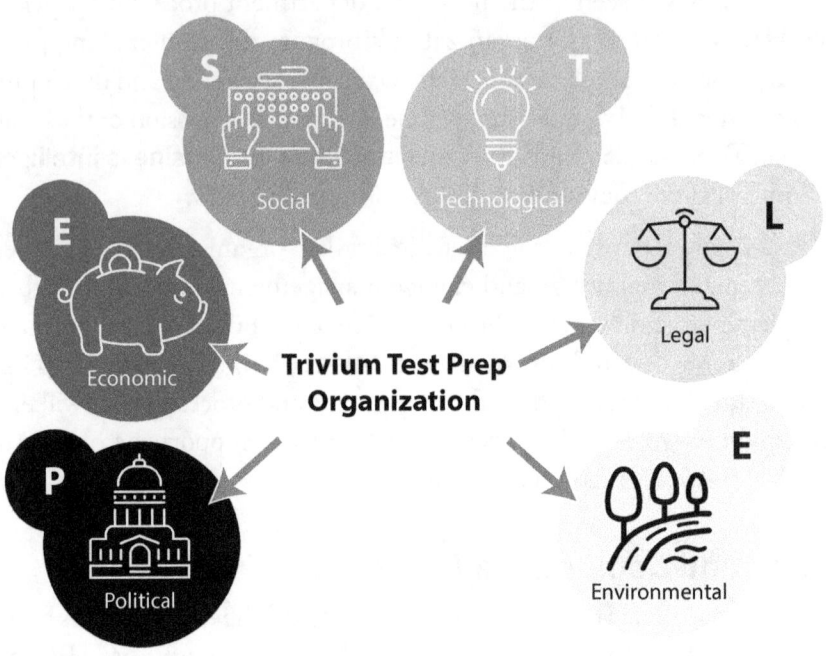

Figure 1.1. PESTLE Analysis

Another tool is **Porter's Five Forces**. In his 1979 article "How Competitive Forces Shape Strategy," Harvard Business School professor Michael E. Porter described five forces to better understand an industry and ensure an organization stays competitive and relevant. Human resources must, along with other functions within the organization, access these forces to proactively develop strategic initiatives. Porter's Five Forces include:

1. competition (rivalry)
2. the potential threat of new entrants to an industry
3. the power of suppliers
4. the power of consumers
5. the threat of substitute products

These forces shape industries and show their strengths and weaknesses.

Competition, or competitive rivalry, refers to competition within an industry. Profit hinges on competition. Even dominant companies in an industry face competition. All companies must be alert to the potential threat of new entrants to an industry. New entrants—new competition—could take away from profits. For example, millions of people went to Blockbuster Video every weekend to rent movies until Netflix pioneered a new model of video rentals.

Still, new entrants to an industry face barriers to entry. Porter discusses six barriers to entry: economies of scale, product differentiation, capital requirements, cost disadvantages relative to size, access to distribution channels, and government policy.

The power of suppliers and the power of consumers (or buyers) refers to the bargaining power of both. Suppliers are powerful, or have strong bargaining power, when they control a product by reducing supply or raising prices. For example, in 1973 the Organization of Petroleum Exporting Countries (OPEC) placed an embargo on the United States, refusing to export oil and causing a gas shortage. Consumers are powerful when they demand higher quality or service. Consumer shift in demand can also force down prices: Consider discounts on Halloween candy in November or Easter candy the week after the holiday.

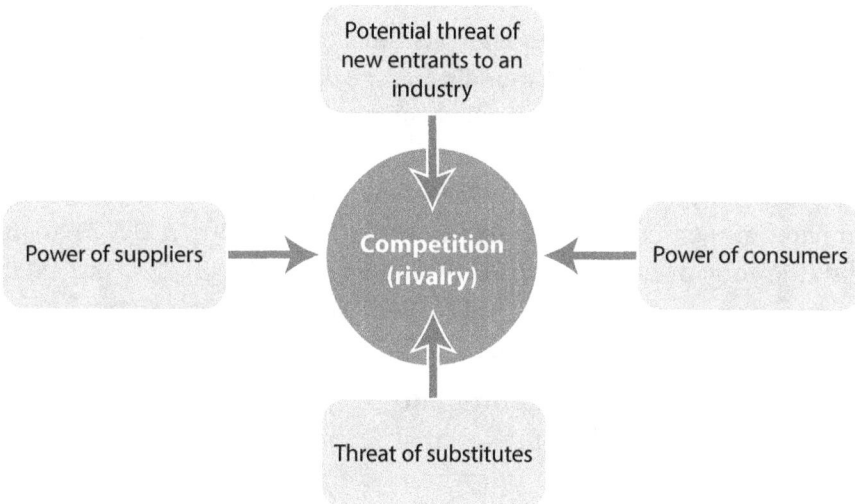

Figure 1.2. Porter's Five Forces

Finally, companies must address the threat of substitute products (or services). Substitute products take away market share and threaten profits. Apple produces the iPhone but must contend with Samsung's Android.

How do business and economic considerations affect HR? When the economy is strong, consumers can afford more products and services. Companies thrive if they meet the demands of consumers. Companies often expand their staff to meet that demand. On the other hand, when the economy is stagnant or in decline, consumers buy fewer products and services. Consequently, companies may have to reduce production costs to offset the loss of profits and lay off employees.

Consumer demand can affect economic conditions for companies as demand for specific products increases or decreases. Over time, consumers develop new tastes, attitudes, and behaviors. What may have been popular with consumers a decade ago may not be today. Therefore, to meet consumer demand, companies refine their existing products and services and develop new ones. This process also affects staffing practices.

Still, organizations must look beyond economics. Local, state, and federal governments and agencies constantly implement new laws and regulations, which inform how a company compensates and treats employees, and how it operates. Depending on where the company conducts business, it may have to follow rules in different locations and keep up with the changing legal landscape in each place.

It is strategically advantageous for any organization to follow developments in technology. The organization may benefit from new technology that streamlines operations and increases efficiency. Finally, an organization should try to attract the most qualified people to fulfill its goals and to remain a desirable place to work. The talent and skills of individuals within the workforce are critical to the success of all organizations.

Business Analysis

HR professionals use **business analysis** tools to maintain business and competitive awareness. **Statistical models** analyze data to uncover trends affecting the organization. For example, an **environmental scan** analyzes external and internal conditions that impact an organization. Another valuable tool is the SWOT analysis, developed by business and management consultant Albert Humphrey at the Stanford Research Institute in the 1960s. A **SWOT analysis** looks at an organization's internal **S**trengths and **W**eaknesses, and external **O**pportunities and **T**hreats. A SWOT analysis reveals important factors to consider before making a decision.

> **HELPFUL HINT**
>
> Conduct a SWOT analysis before setting objectives. The SWOT analysis will show if an objective is realistic and achievable.

These factors are broken down into four quadrants to visualize the internal and external landscape. Opportunities and threats are always external and cannot be controlled. They can, however, be planned for. Strengths and weaknesses are internal and can be controlled. In addition, strengths and opportunities can help overcome weaknesses and threats.

HR uses these tools to track outcomes, costs, and ROI of HR initiatives and programs. HR dashboards track and monitor **key performance indicators (KPIs)**. KPIs should be relevant to the business and impact profitability. For instance, an organization that hires only a few people a year might choose to monitor and manage the costs of training efforts or benefit programs. However, if an organization hires a large number of employees due to growth or turnover, then KPIs such as time to hire or cost of hire would be strategically important.

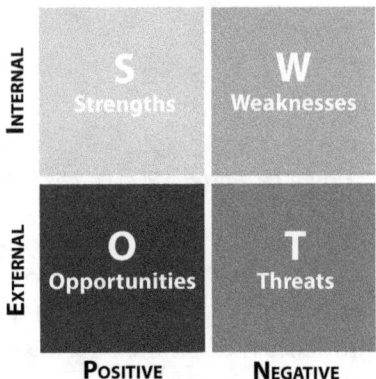

Figure 1.3. SWOT Analysis

Through KPIs, HR speaks the language of business by showing the results of programs through data and dollars. KPIs are used not only for measuring the success of past programs but also for developing and planning for the future.

The **Human Resource Information System (HRIS)** is an electronic platform for data entry, tracking, and reporting human resources information. The system maintains important static information about employees like addresses, social security numbers, tax withholding information, job and pay information, and benefit elections. The HRIS can typically produce static reports such as employee lists, as well as analytical reports like turnover, headcount, and other information useful for planning purposes. HRIS vendors package their systems with various capabilities, and some are more robust than others. Typically, an HRIS will provide the organization with:

- the ability to manage all employee information and records
- the ability to track applicants
- reporting capabilities on HR metrics
- the ability to post HR documents such as employee handbooks, procedures, and forms
- benefits administration
- integration with payroll or other HR management systems

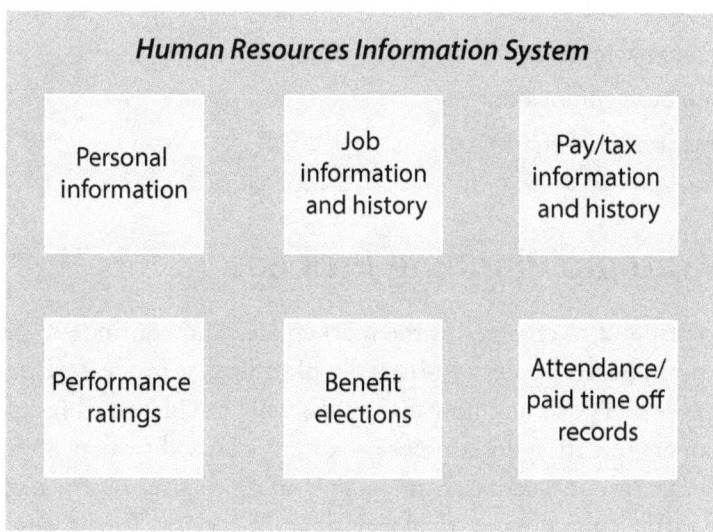

Figure 1.4. Information Collected in HRIS

The HRIS should provide data the company needs to track and analyze applicants, employees, and former employees. Some systems allow employees to update their own basic information (like address changes or tax withholdings) and benefit enrollments. HR staff can then focus on strategic functions rather than administrative data entry. Some more robust HRIS systems also allow organizations to conduct performance reviews within the system to allow for easy dissemination, collection, and tracking. The data collected in an HRIS can be used to make employment decisions like merit increases, promotions, and restructuring. Managers can also access information to effectively support the success of their direct reports.

HRIS systems are often integrated with other HR functional systems like an applicant tracker or learning management system. With an **applicant tracking system (ATS)**, the employer can post jobs and collect candidates within one system. An ATS typically allows for candidate assessments and the sharing of candidates with the hiring manager. A **learning management system (LMS)**, like the ATS, is a platform with one location for the creation, distribution, and record retention of training and development within the organization. Using these systems allows seamless integration of static employee information along with a common platform for access and storage of information.

HRIS professionals maintain all personnel (and sometimes payroll) records, including employee names, addresses, emergency contacts, job and pay information, performance ratings, leaves of absence, benefit elections, and more. They also provide reports to leaders and managers to support personnel decisions or to monitor employee metrics (e.g., turnover). HRIS functions may be managed by an HRIS specialist, a departmental assistant, an HR generalist, or another specialist.

EXAMPLE

3. Which of the following is examined during a PESTLE analysis?
   A) turnover rate
   B) economic factors
   C) employee complaints
   D) organizational charts

The Strategic Planning Process

In order to respond to changes in the marketplace and continue to grow, organizations periodically undergo **strategic planning**, a process of defining its overall purpose and goals and how these goals will be achieved. Through strategic planning, an organization determines its current status, direction, approach, and how it will measure its success. Strategic planning focuses on the organization as a whole rather than on a particular product or service. The process, which is generally carried out on a periodic basis, answers the following questions about the organization:

1. Where are we now?
2. Where do we want to be in ____ years?
3. How will we get there?
4. How will we know when we are there?

There are several approaches to strategic planning that may be tailored to the unique needs of the organization depending on its size, leadership, maturity level, and culture:

- **Goals-based planning** focuses on the organization's mission, vision, and values. Goals are set to achieve the mission; the steps needed to achieve the goals are determined.
- **Issues-based planning** focuses on the issues facing the organization and determines the steps needed to address those issues.
- **Organic planning** focuses on a common vision and values and identifying best practices and methodologies in the organization. The stakeholders focus on what is already working rather than fixing problems.

Regardless of the method, strategic plans are typically developed for a period of one year or more. Some plans may be in-depth, with step-by-step actions, while others are high-level with no steps. In general, though, the strategic planning process has the following elements:

1. **Plan the process.** Stakeholders decide on process, participants, and time frame. Preplanning reduces errors in the planning process and achieves commitment from leaders.
2. **Study the environment.** Stakeholders use tools like statistical models, SWOT analysis, PESTLE analysis, and Porter's Five Forces to determine the organization's present state.
3. **Formulate a strategy.** Stakeholders develop the organization's mission, vision, values, goals, and objectives; they focus on the future and the organization's direction or destination.
4. **Implement the strategy.** Stakeholders articulate goals, develop budgets, create action plans, and execute plans.
5. **Evaluate the strategy.** Stakeholders evaluate the strategy periodically and make adjustments.

The formal strategic plan, however, is not as important as the process itself, or as the execution of the plan. An organization gains many benefits through the strategic planning process, including:

- creating a sense of purpose
- helping leadership set goals
- enhancing communication with staff
- keeping staff involved
- enabling leadership to allocate resources appropriately
- creating accountability
- building consensus

Uniting stakeholders to discuss the future of the organization is a healthy process that will keep it adaptable to change and viable in the marketplace. Leveraging the existing organizational hierarchy to execute the plan and reviewing progress periodically are keys to successfully implementing the strategic plan.

Mission, Vision, and Values

During the strategic planning process, an organization typically reviews its mission, vision, and values statements.

- A **mission statement** defines the organization's purpose, what it offers, whom it serves, and where it operates.
- A **vision statement** outlines the organization's goals.
- An organization's **core values** frame its perspective and guide its actions.

If the organization has not already created these, or is doing so for the first time, it typically will develop these statements as part of the strategic planning process. Once these statements are formalized, the organization develops goals to support them. These statements help stakeholders and employees maintain focus during the strategic planning process and throughout the year.

HR plays an important role in the strategic planning process. HR professionals help create and decide on HR initiatives. HR is also instrumental in communicating and disseminating the strategic plan to employees so that everyone within the organization can understand and support key initiatives. Additionally, through talent management and development, HR ensures that the organization is staffed with skilled individuals who move the strategic plan forward.

Developing Goals

When developing goals, leadership must define not only the goal but also the desired results. An organization's goals should be **SMART**:

- **S**pecific: goals must be clear and detailed enough to guide action plans.
- **M**easurable: goals require metrics to determine their progress.
- **A**ction-oriented: goals should describe the actions needed to accomplish them.
- **R**ealistic: goals should be achievable.
- **T**ime-based: goals require a time frame for completion.

HR can play a key role in goal development by working with individuals, departments, and the organization to roll out SMART goals and train staff in achieving them.

Implementing the Strategic Plan

Once the strategic plan has been developed, organizational leaders, including HR, will consult with department heads, management, and other key employees to begin the implementation process. Implementation includes developing tactical goals and action plans, which can be specific to departments, work groups, or even certain individuals in the organization. The tactical goals and action plans should tie directly to the more broadly stated strategic plan and should be SMART.

After the goals and action plans are developed, leadership and management will address budgetary issues and resources needed to achieve the strategic plan. The organization may decide it needs additional personnel, new technology, or external assistance. Those involved in the budgeting process will make recommendations on what cash and resources are needed, and leadership will determine whether these recommendations support the strategic plan.

Evaluating the Strategic Plan

Strategic planning does not end with the development of that plan. Rather, the process continues throughout the year or years. As the organization implements its plan, it should periodically evaluate whether it is on track to achieve the strategic goals. This includes evaluating the tactical goals and action plans as well. If the organization's leaders find that the organization is not on track, they may decide to revise the action plan or tactical goals or even to reevaluate the strategic plan itself. Sometimes, internal or external factors may cause an organization to change course. Organizations that can adapt accordingly to their environment are likely to succeed.

The Role of HR in Strategic Planning

HR leaders have an important role in the strategic planning process. HR develops its own goals and action plans that align with the overarching goals of the organization. The strategic HR plan—or **human capital plan**—addresses the same questions raised during the larger strategic planning process. As with any strategic plan, the strategic HR plan will differ from organization to organization. However, there are some commonalities, as listed in table 1.2:

TABLE 1.2. Components of a Human Capital Plan	
COMPONENT	EXPLANATION
Strategic direction	Strategic direction requires knowledge of the organization's strategic plans; budgetary constraints; internal and external forces affecting human capital; makeup of the current workforce; and customer and stakeholder expectations, challenges, and needs. HR must develop a vision of the future workforce to determine the ideal human capital necessary for the organization to achieve its strategic goals.
Human capital goals	Human capital goals are related to the organization's talent (employees), performance management, and leadership. Goals may relate to the hiring, training, and allocation of employees to achieve certain objectives in the organization's general strategic plan.
Strategies for accomplishing goals	These strategies specifically describe how goals will be achieved. Consideration should be given to the availability and capabilities of human capital.
Implementation plan	The implementation plan describes the actions needed to accomplish goals and objectives. Implementation plans include the following components: • a description of each task necessary to carry out the objectives • stakeholders responsible for each task • resources required (e.g., human, financial) • time frames (e.g., milestones, deadlines)
Communications plan	The communications plan describes how key stakeholders in the organization will stay informed about the progress of the strategic plan and the actions they need to take. HR must communicate regularly with all stakeholders to ensure their understanding of the plan and to solicit feedback. The communications plan is often a subset of the implementation plan.
Accountability system	The accountability system measures and tracks progress in executing the strategy or objective. People and teams identified in the implementation plan are held accountable. Specific targets are identified by describing the level of performance or rate of improvement needed for each part of the implementation plan. Establishing metrics provides essential direction to those involved in executing the objectives and shows progress of the plan's implementation.

First, human resources leadership establishes a human capital management plan. Then it develops a budget to implement the plan. Depending on finances, the human resources departmental budget may include these costs:

- employee compensation (salaries, bonuses, and benefits)
- payroll taxes
- equipment and supplies
- training and development fees
- travel
- outsourced services (e.g., payroll, benefits administration, HRIS)

HR may also lead the development of budgetary items that are then allocated to other departments or verticals in the organization. These costs may include:

- recruitment fees
- training and development fees
- raises
- employee incentives or awards
- temporary staff

In some cases, it may be more cost-effective to outsource functions or repurpose HR positions to carry out new or different tasks. Furthermore, some processes can be streamlined so that HR personnel can focus on tasks that are more impactful to the organization.

Managing Organizational Change

As a result of the strategic planning process, an organization may decide that it needs to restructure itself in order to achieve its goals and remain competitive and viable in the marketplace. Organizational leadership may decide to explore or implement any of a number of structural changes.

In **restructuring** or reengineering, leadership may examine processes for redundancy within the entire organization or in certain departments or teams; it may also simplify operations to improve efficiency and reduce costs.

With an **expansion in force**, an organization grows teams by creating new positions and hiring additional personnel. This may lead to a culture clash between veteran employees and newcomers. It will also require resources to train the new employees and acclimate them to the new environment.

Conversely, a **reduction in force** decreases personnel expense by eliminating positions or departments. Also called **downsizing**, this may create anxiety for remaining employees, who must take on the extra workload while feeling uncertain about the security of their own jobs.

Mergers and acquisitions (M&As) are a combination of two or more entities. In a merger, two companies combine to leverage both of their assets while forming a new, stronger corporate identity. Acquisitions involve a larger company purchasing another company and integrating it into the existing culture and operations. With **divestiture**, a company's product line, service, or business unit is spun off or sold. Typically, the existing team involved in the divestiture remains intact.

In **outsourcing**, the organization uses external service providers to handle certain business functions, such as accounting, payroll, or IT. Finally, **offshoring** is when an organization moves certain jobs or functions to other countries where labor is cheaper. This has other implications, such as a loss of jobs elsewhere, cultural barriers, and time zone differences.

All employees are affected by organizational change in some way. In some cases, their responsibilities may increase or change. Others may worry about losing their jobs. Unfortunately, some employees will lose their jobs. HR professionals help manage organizational change by establishing programs and communications to help employees understand changes, manage their emotions, and adapt to restructuring.

It is important for the organization to communicate regularly with employees about the changes, let them know how they are affected, and be truthful about the facts. If the organization is not truthful, or if employees perceive that information is being withheld, it risks losing longer-term employees with valuable historical knowledge. Decreased productivity could be the consequence.

EXAMPLES

4. Strategic planning is centered around the organization's
    A) staffing plan.
    B) mission statement.
    C) needs analysis.
    D) competitor data.

5. To be effective, company goals must
    A) require the participation of line staff.
    B) be available in multiple languages.
    C) grow the company.
    D) be specific and measurable.

Navigating the Organization

Structures of Organizations

Every company is organized differently depending on industry, size, tax implications, and leadership. However, all businesses operating in the United States are formally organized into one of four basic structures.

Sole proprietorships are the most basic business structure. In sole proprietorships, the business owner operates alone as the sole responsible party for the business (including finances); he or she has the sole authority to make business decisions. Any profits made by the business belong to the owner, who is personally responsible for all debts and liabilities of the company. Many business owners of a sole proprietorship operate the company through an assumed name registered with the county or state in which they operate.

In a **partnership**, two or more people share ownership of the business. Partnerships take various forms such as a general partnership, limited liability partnership, or a joint venture, depending on the structure of ownership as well as the intended duration of the partnership. Many partnerships have formal agreements that outline how profits will be divided, how disputes will be resolved, how change in ownership may occur, and how the partnership may be dissolved.

A **corporation** is a legal entity owned by shareholders in the form of stock or equity. Corporations are most commonly formed for large businesses. Unlike sole proprietorships and partnerships, the corporation itself (not the shareholders or owners) is liable for the actions and debts of the business. Shareholders are typically not involved in the daily operations of the business. Instead, they elect a board of directors to represent their interests, and the company's senior leadership team makes decisions about the direction of the company.

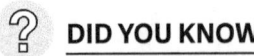

DID YOU KNOW?

Both an LLC and a C-corp can file for an S-corp status through the IRS. The **S-corp** designation means the entity will be taxed as a partnership and will therefore avoid double taxation, which happens when tax is paid on both the business and the owner's incomes.

Finally, a **limited liability company (LLC)** is a hybrid of a partnership and a corporation. LLCs provide the liability protections of a corporation while offering the simplified tax implications of a partnership. The "owners" of an LLC are called "members," and depending on the state, there can be one or more members.

Design and designation of a corporation or company depends on the desired tax implications. Typically, the LLC itself does not pay taxes. Instead, the taxes pass through to the member's personal tax filing. C-corporations, or **C-corps**, on the other hand, are taxed separately from the owner or shareholders. That is, the organization itself is subject to corporate income taxation.

Operational Functions in an Organization

Regardless of size and formal structure, most organizations need certain **core functions** to operate. Below are the general business functions that contribute to achieving the organization's objective:

- **Procurement, Logistics, and Distribution** professionals acquire resources (inputs) and deliver final products to customers.
- **Product or Service Development** professionals design, revise, and improve products or services offered to the marketplace; their duties may include research, design, analysis, and engineering.
- **Operations** professionals and teams organize raw products and production processes to create a final product or service; they also determine methods for cost savings.
- **Marketing and Sales** professionals target prospective clients, develop and maintain relationships with existing customers, and promote and advertise products and services through multiple channels.
- **Customer Service** representatives support customers who buy products or services, resolve problems and complaints, and answer questions about products or services.

The following are **support functions**:

- **General Management** oversees corporate governance, accounting, facilities, management, and administrative support.
- **Human Resources** professionals oversee the recruitment, hiring, training, compensation, and termination of employees.
- **Information Technology** professionals maintain, automate, and design the technical infrastructure of the organization, including equipment, hardware, and software.

Depending on the complexity and size of the organization, these functions may be handled by one person or multiple people. All are necessary components for conducting business.

Organizational Design and Development

Organizational design aligns people, processes, compensation, and metrics with the strategy of the organization to ensure that the organization embodies its core values as specified in its vision statement. The design reflects the organization's need to respond to changes (internal and external); integrate new people, technologies, and processes; encourage collaboration; and offer flexibility.

A company can be organized in different ways, depending on its objectives. Leaders and managers must decide how to group people together so they can perform their work effectively. There are five common approaches to organizational design that help decision-makers group people (i.e., positions) together in the organization.

1. **Functional structure** groups positions into departments or units based on similar tasks, expertise, skills, and resources. Groups within a functional structure include accounting and finance, human resources, information technology, and marketing.
2. **Divisional structure** groups business units according to a type of output. For example, units may be aligned with specific geographic locales, products, or clients.
3. **Matrix structure** mixes functional and divisional structure. People work in teams that integrate disparate expertise. Employees working in a matrix structure belong to both a functional and a divisional group (e.g., a project team or product team).
4. **Team structure** integrates separate functions into a group based on a particular goal or objective. Teams foster collaboration, cooperation, problem-solving, and relationship-building among various functions.
5. **Network structure** involves external entities performing certain functions on a temporary or contractual basis. Work is assigned, for example, to a contractor for a period of time in order to achieve a certain goal.

Organizational structures evolve over time due to organizational growth, environmental change, and other circumstances. The strategic planning process identifies ways to maintain a sound structure that positions the organization to achieve its goals and objectives. The organization's structure should support what it hopes to achieve. Otherwise, the organization will be at a disadvantage and may risk losing its competitiveness.

Centralized versus Decentralized Decision-Making

In addition to the physical structure of the organization, it is important to consider the structure of decision-making. Decisions are constantly being made: whom to hire, what products or services to offer, where to operate, what clients to target, and more. Decision-making in an organization can be either centralized or decentralized.

Centralized organizational structures depend on one individual (or group of executives) to make decisions and provide direction. Smaller organizations often use this structure because the owner is responsible for the company's business operations. As a benefit, centralized organizations often experience quick, efficient decision-making. Business owners typically set the company's mission, vision, goals, and objectives, which managers are expected to support and execute. However, centralized organizations can become bureaucratic as they grow, due to the hierarchy of management leading to the owner. Accomplishing tasks takes longer, resulting in slower operations and lower productivity.

Decentralized organizational structures, on the other hand, often have several individuals responsible for management decisions. Decentralized organizations depend on a team environment at different levels of the business in order to make decisions. (Individuals may have some autonomy to make business decisions but generally must align with the vision of the larger group.) Decentralized organizations typically employ individuals with a variety of knowledge and skills, ensuring that the company can handle various types of business situations. However, reaching consensus among decision-makers in decentralized organizations can be challenging. This can slow the organization's progress in achieving its objectives and harm productivity.

Organizational leadership should carefully consider work styles, personalities, goals, vision, and overall environment when choosing the right structure for the organization. Small organizations typically adopt centralized decision-making structures because owners often remain at the forefront of business operations. Larger organizations often use a more decentralized structure because they have several divisions or departments. Additionally, business leaders may consider changing organizational structure depending on the growth of the business and overall strategy.

Distribution and Coordination of Labor

Regardless of their structure, all organizations are groups of people working together toward a common goal. To efficiently accomplish their goals, organizations typically divide work into manageable parts. They also coordinate the work so that all employees are working interdependently toward the same objectives.

Division of labor refers to the distribution of work into separate jobs that are performed by different people. Division of labor leads to **job specialization** as workers focus on one or a few tasks now essential to their positions. As companies grow over time, horizontal division of labor (many people doing similar jobs) is usually accompanied by a vertical division of labor (a hierarchy of managers and supervisors overseeing jobs performed). Job specialization also increases work efficiency.

Workers can master smaller tasks quickly, and less time is wasted changing from one task to another. Training costs are also reduced because employees require fewer skills to accomplish the work. Finally, job specialization makes it easier to recruit and hire people best suited for the specific jobs. However, an organization's ability to divide work among employees depends on how well those people can collaborate and work with each other. Otherwise, productivity suffers due to the misallocation of tasks or resources, or duplication of effort.

Coordination tends to become more challenging as jobs become more specialized. Therefore, companies typically specialize jobs so that coordination is possible. Every organization coordinates work via informal communication, formal hierarchy, or standardization.

Types of informal communication include sharing information with other employees through face-to-face interaction, email, and conference calls. Team meetings are a common method of informal communication, where tactical matters are discussed and work is coordinated at a more specific level. Hierarchy gives authority to individuals at certain levels of the organization, who then direct work processes and allocate resources. This is also known as the chain of command. Standardization is the development of routine processes, measured outputs, and required training or competencies.

Span of Control

Span of control describes the extent of a manager's authority: the number of employees reporting to him or her. A few employees reporting to each manager results in a narrow span of control and a lengthy hierarchical structure—this is known as a tall organization. On the other hand, many employees reporting to each manager results in a wide span of control, creating a flat organization. Because it is determined by so many factors, span of control is helpful in understanding organizational design and behaviors.

One factor is organizational size; due to costs, large organizations tend to have a narrow span of control, while smaller organizations typically have a wider span of control. Required job skills must also be considered: Tasks involving fewer skills will require less supervision, resulting in a wider span of control. Complex tasks may need a narrower span of control, so supervisors can provide more individualized attention.

Another factor is organizational culture; flexible workplaces typically have a wider span of control because the organization provides a more autonomous environment in which employees need little supervision. Finally, manager workload is a key factor. Managers should be able to plan departmental activities, train staff, and manage performance while being accountable for their own responsibilities.

Spans of control can be purposefully widened by giving workers more autonomy and holding them accountable to manage themselves. Standardizing the work processes of junior employees to avoid costly mistakes will also widen the span of control. As the span of control widens in an organization, the number of relationships among managers grows too.

EXAMPLE

6. Decentralization works best in organizations where
    A) employees dislike management.
    B) unions are present.
    C) a quick response to problems is needed.
    D) the organization is too top-heavy.

Organizational Change and Growth

Like people, organizations have their own **life cycles**. They are "born" (established), they develop and mature, they decline, and sometimes they "die" (dissolve). Just like people, as organizations mature, they begin to understand the environment around them, develop knowledge and wisdom, and plan for the future. Organizations at any stage of the life cycle are impacted by both internal and external factors. In order to survive, an organization must adapt to changes, demands, and its internal and external environment.

According to scholar Richard L. Daft, an expert in organization behavior and design, as an organization progresses through its life cycle and grows in size, its functions and features evolve over time:

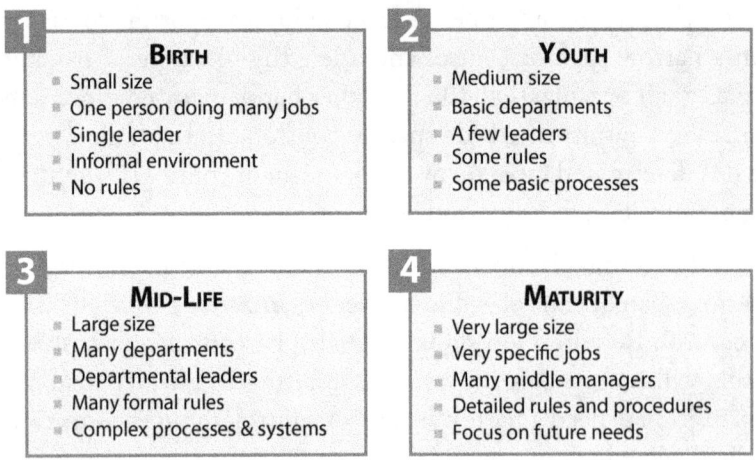

Figure 1.5. The Life Cycle of a Company

Growth Phases

In 1972, organizational development scholar Larry E. Greiner conceptualized five **growth phases** an organization undergoes: growth through creativity, direction, delegation, coordination, and collaboration. According to Greiner, each growth phase is a period of organizational evolution of four to eight years followed by a period of organizational crisis. The phases and the expected crises that result, according to his theory, are listed in greater detail below:

TABLE 1.3. Growth Phases of an Organization

GROWTH PHASE	RESULTING CRISIS	ORGANIZATIONAL NEEDS	ACTION TO BE TAKEN
Growth through creativity	crisis of leadership	More formalized management practices are needed.	Leaders must adapt practices or hire managers to assume this authority.
Growth through direction	crisis of autonomy	Lower-level managers need more authority.	Leaders must delegate authority.
Growth through delegation	crisis of control	Employees need autonomy to do jobs, while leaders need to feel in control.	Leaders must develop a system of checks and balances.
Growth through coordination	crisis of bureaucracy	Focus groups, planning processes, and staff cause delays in decision-making; innovation suffers.	Management must develop collaborative teams and break down silos.
Growth through collaboration	No formal crisis is indicated. However, employees may grow exhausted by teamwork and pressure.		

Effective leaders are aware of the growth phases of the organization and plan accordingly, typically through the strategic planning process (discussed in detail below). Understanding where the organization lies in the growth cycle also helps leaders respond appropriately to problems and crises and make decisions more efficiently. As organizations progress through the life cycle, it is important for leaders to manage change in order to ensure that management and staff are closely aligned with the strategic vision and objectives, in order for them to be carried out effectively.

Not all organizations are able to survive the growth phase in its entirety. Some may collapse due to an inability to respond to changes and demands. Others may be acquired by another company and therefore cease to operate autonomously. If an organization does successfully progress through the growth phases, it will reach a point of maturity and eventually decline.

Maturity and Decline

An organization has reached maturity once it has resources to plan for the future, formalized policies and procedures, and a solid infrastructure in which it operates. In this stage of the organizational life cycle, it is typical for organizations to become bureaucratic, making it more difficult to make decisions or change direction quickly. Bureaucratization harms the organization if its competition or industry evolves at a rapid pace (e.g., by developing new products and services).

On the other hand, an organization in the maturity phase also experiences stability. Functional departments and formalized procedures make hiring and training staff easier. Additionally, mature organizations also have the financial resources and planning necessary to pay their employees competitively. The phase of maturity may last for several years or decades as long as the organization is able to respond to crises and changes in the environment.

Once an organization has reached a high level of inefficiency and bureaucracy, it will begin to decline. The organization's products or services may be outdated, and sales may decline due to a lack of innovation. Leadership may respond by reducing the workforce, closing facilities, or finding other cost-cutting measures that reduce redundancy. To revive the organization, leaders must innovate by developing new or refined products or services that meet the demands of the marketplace. Otherwise, the organization may fail and cease to exist, or it may be acquired by a larger organization in a growth phase.

EXAMPLES

7. What is a sign that an organization has reached maturity?
   A) It has formalized policies and procedures.
   B) It has a high level of inefficiency and bureaucracy.
   C) Leadership reduces the workforce.
   D) Bureaucratization harms innovation.

8. An organization has many detailed procedures and is resistant to change. Which phase of the organizational life cycle does this describe?
   A) birth
   B) growth
   C) maturity
   D) decline

Mergers and Acquisitions

When a company undergoes a merger or acquisition, the human resources department is a valuable partner in the process. In **mergers and acquisitions**

(M&As), an organization combines with or is absorbed by another organization. HR helps the organization conduct its due diligence when evaluating a potential merger, plan a strategy for integrating the other company's employees, and manage the change process. HR can conduct a risk assessment to identify possible conflicts before an M&A to address any problems. Given the complex nature of M&As, human resources can provide particular expertise in several areas.

Evaluating Company Culture

Every company has its own unique culture, and when two companies combine (through a merger or acquisition), employees may experience culture shock. When a company is considering a merger or acquisition, its human resources department should evaluate the other company's culture and analyze how well that company would integrate with the other. HR processes and recognizing cultural differences should happen during the merger.

Organizational culture affects how employees work; what benefits they receive; the formality of the workplace; management methods; and shared work styles, attitudes, and values. HR uses the discovery process to determine this information; in this process, policies, procedures, communications, and other important documents are confidentially shared and evaluated. If there are significant differences between the two organizations, they should be thoroughly addressed prior to the merger or acquisition.

Identifying Compensation and Benefits Issues

During the due diligence process, the purchasing organization must also determine whether the deal makes financial sense. Part of the financial data includes compensation and benefits. HR should review the compensation structures and benefit plans the other company offers. It should identify whether the compensation structures and pay levels are compatible with that of the purchasing organization. It should also determine whether there are any inconsistencies between the benefit plans, such as a difference in premium costs, coverage levels, or funding of retirement plans (e.g., company match on a 401(k) plan).

Managing Change

Change is not easy for most people. When a merger or acquisition occurs, employees may experience anxiety about their job security or the future in general. HR can help alleviate some of this anxiety by communicating regularly with employees, being responsive to their questions, and being open to feedback. HR should monitor employee morale and identify any challenges, fears, or rumors that arise due to the M&A. HR can help alleviate uncertainty, dispel rumors, and make the transition smoother.

Organizational Design and Development

When one company merges with or acquires another, some functions or jobs may be consolidated due to redundancy. **Workforce optimization**, the process of maximizing an organization's resources to achieve optimum performance, typically happens after the merger. Workforce optimization may include downsizing in the event of a talent surplus. Downsizing is a feature of some M&As. This process may happen quickly or over a longer period of time. HR plays an active role in restructuring the organization, identifying ways to work more efficiently and evaluating the impact of change. HR professionals are responsible for communicating changes to employees, revising job descriptions, handling difficult situations (such as layoffs or resistance to change), offering training as necessary, and motivating employees.

EXAMPLE

9. What is the planned elimination of personnel to streamline operations?
    - A) acquisition
    - B) consolidation
    - C) termination
    - D) downsizing

Ethics

HR professionals play a key role in ensuring the integrity of organizations. HR is often the advocate, gatekeeper, and communicator of the ethical standards. HR professionals must meet the highest standards of interpreting and overseeing corporate and legal policies. The organization and employees look to HR to be fair and to administer policies with principles.

HR is also involved in a company's ethics by supporting the establishment and institution of guidelines, policies, and procedures that govern behavior within a business. This may be through creating guiding principles or values that are communicated throughout the organization. By articulating how an organization desires to do business, employees, clients, and customers have a shared understanding of culture and beliefs that guide their actions and decision-making.

Corporate Governance

Corporate governance refers to the set of systems, principles, and processes that guide everything a company does, including the relationships between its stakeholders (board of directors, management, and others).

Corporate governance is based on transparency, integrity, fairness, compliance, accountability, and responsibility. An active, independent board of directors provides corporate oversight and represents shareholders' interests. The board of directors typically includes inside directors (who work for the organization) and outside directors (who do not work for the organization). The board is elected by the shareholders (who are owners of the corporation). Management, including executives, are employees of the organization and oversee the daily operations of the organization.

Although a corporation is a legal entity, it cannot make a decision for itself. Instead, the board of directors and management make decisions for the organization. These stakeholders have a fiduciary responsibility to the organization, meaning their decisions should be in the best interests of stakeholders and the organization's survival. Of course, this does not always happen. In response to corporate scandals in the early 2000s by Enron and WorldCom, among others, the Sarbanes–Oxley Act was enacted in 2002 to ensure that stakeholders in public corporations appropriately maintain and uphold their fiduciary responsibilities.

The Sarbanes–Oxley Act of 2002

The **Sarbanes–Oxley Act** addresses unethical practices in public corporations and enforces penalties for violations. Its provisions include the following:

1. The Public Company Accounting Oversight Board was developed to require all public accounting firms to register with the board, which could audit the company's records for compliance.
2. Standards were established to maintain the independent nature of auditors. Results of audits (including recommendations) are now provided directly to the audit committee of the organization's board of directors.
3. Standards for corporate responsibility were established, and the organization's chief executive is held accountable for the accuracy of filings with the **Securities and Exchange Commission**.
4. CEOs and CFOs are required to forfeit bonuses or gains through shares of stock for a one-year period when the organization files a restatement of financial reports with the SEC due to misconduct.
5. Insider trading of stock is prohibited during pension fund blackout periods.
6. CFOs must satisfy certain ethical requirements.
7. Management officials who commit fraud or obstruct justice face criminal penalties.
8. Whistleblowers who report misconduct they reasonably believe to violate SEC regulations or federal laws are protected.

Corporate Ethics

Ethical behavior begins at the highest levels of an organization. When the organization's directors, officers, and managers show their commitment to behaving ethically, employees are prone to follow their example. Many organizations, whether or not they are subject to compliance with Sarbanes–Oxley, demonstrate their commitment to corporate responsibility by developing organization-wide ethics statements, values statements, and codes of conduct.

- A **code of ethics** is an organization's ideals—what it wants to do when conducting business.

- A **code of conduct** is what an organization expects from employees; it also lays out how those who violate this code will be disciplined.

Within the code of conduct, the organization should indicate how conflicts of interest, insider information, and gifts should be handled. **Conflicts of interest** arise when an employee might personally benefit from the action of the organization. Typically, the employee is required to disclose potential conflicts of interest, and management will identify ways to avoid or mitigate the conflict.

Gifts from vendors or clients to an employee in the organization are a type of conflict of interest identified in such a policy. Insider information can lead to a conflict of interest when the employee has access to information that the general public does not have. Using insider information to make decisions on the purchase or sale of stock is prohibited by law and carries criminal and civil penalties.

Whistleblower Protection

Under the Sarbanes–Oxley Act, violations of securities laws or a breach of fiduciary duty must be reported to the chief legal officer or CEO of the organization. An organization's legal team (in-house or external counsel) must also report these violations to the organization's board of directors audit committee. The Sarbanes–Oxley Act provides protections for people who, in good faith, report suspected or witnessed wrongdoing. These people are called **whistleblowers**; they report violations, assist those reporting violations, and help with investigations.

Whistleblower protections are regulated by the Department of Labor and the Occupational Safety and Health Administration (OSHA). Under OSHA regulations, an employer is prohibited from taking adverse action against whistleblowers, including termination of employment, reducing pay, discipline, intimidation, coercion, or any other type of retaliation. Publicly traded companies are required by Sarbanes–Oxley to establish confidential whistleblower complaints and to maintain those records according to the rules established in the law. Organizations that are not publicly traded (and therefore not subject to Sarbanes–Oxley) may elect, at their own will, to establish whistleblower policies and procedures in order to maintain an ethical workplace.

Ethics Officers

Organizations committed to maintaining ethical standards often choose a key person to serve as an ethics officer. This may be a person at the executive level, the company's internal legal counsel, or the highest-ranking human resources professional. Ethics officers advise all employees in the organization on their obligations to maintain an ethical workplace, including acceptable and unacceptable conduct. They oversee the training of all employees on ethical matters; they also develop policies to maintain compliance with Sarbanes–Oxley (as applicable) and consistency with corporate values and ethics. Finally, ethics officers consult with other organizational leaders on ethical issues.

Within an organization, HR leaders are often asked to wear the hat of the ethics officer. This may be more likely in smaller organizations that do not have the resources or means to employ an individual strictly for this role.

EXAMPLE

10. A whistleblower
    - A) cannot expect protection under the law.
    - B) enjoys protection under the Sarbanes–Oxley Act.
    - C) is protected under OSHA regulations.
    - D) is in violation of a company's code of ethics.

Answer Key

1. **C)** An HR specialist has technical knowledge and skills in specific areas.

2. **B)** Employee handbooks should be carefully reviewed and updated regularly because they may create an enforceable contract.

3. **B)** A PESTLE analysis studies Political, Economic, Social, Technological, Legal, and Environmental factors. Economic factors like interest rates, unemployment, and more would be considered during a PESTLE analysis.

4. **B)** Strategic planning focuses on the organization as a whole, and it should be centered around the organization's mission statement.

5. **D)** Goals should be SMART: Specific, Measurable, Action-oriented, Realistic, and Time-based.

6. **C)** Decentralization can aid a quick response to problems, as opposed to centralization, in which accomplishing tasks generally takes longer.

7. **A)** An organization has reached maturity once it has resources to plan for the future, formalized policies and procedures, and a solid infrastructure in which it operates.

8. **D)** An organization with many detailed procedures that is resistant to change could be bureaucratized and in decline.

9. **D)** Downsizing is the planned elimination of personnel to streamline operations. Also known as a "reduction in force," downsizing may accompany M&As.

10. **C)** Whistleblowers are protected under OSHA from pay reduction, discipline, and other forms of retaliation.

2 Leading and Communicating in the Workplace

Leadership

Leadership takes many different forms. Different approaches are appropriate for different circumstances. Several categories of leadership theories have developed since the early twentieth century.

Leadership Theories

Trait theories maintain that effective leaders share common traits, beliefs, and thought processes. Early trait theorists believed that leadership is an innate quality: either a person is naturally a leader, or they are not. Over time, theorists came to understand that people can develop leadership qualities.

Today, trait theories help managers identify qualities (like integrity, charisma, empathy, assertiveness, and problem-solving skills) that help individuals lead others. However, there is no specific combination of traits that makes an ideal leader.

Behavioral theories focus on how leaders act toward others. In the 1930s, leading social psychologist Kurt Lewin discussed the behavior of the leader. According to Lewin, there are three styles of leadership:

1. Autocratic leaders make decisions with little or no input from their subordinates. They dictate what needs to be done and how to do it. Autocratic leadership is useful when quick decisions are needed but input is not.

2. Democratic leaders offer guidance to the team but allow team members to provide input before making a decision. Democratic leadership is effective when team agreement matters. It can be challenging when individual perspectives and ideas clash.

3. Laissez-faire leaders allow team members to make many decisions on their own. This approach works when the team is skilled, motivated, and does not need close supervision. Oversight is still needed to make sure the team stays focused.

Effective managers use a combination of these three styles as appropriate. Leaders should be adaptable based on the needs of their teams and the organization.

Researchers agree there is no one correct type of leader, and that different leadership styles can be used effectively in different situations. **Contingency theories** address the best style for the circumstance. The Hersey-Blanchard model, for example, links leadership style with the maturity of team members (see below). Other contingency-based models include Robert House's path-goal theory, which says that leadership should depend on the team members' needs, the task at hand, and the environment in which they are working.

Power and influence theories consider the different ways leaders use their power and influence to accomplish tasks. Social psychologists John French and Bertram Raven identified five forms of power. **French and Raven's Five Forms of Power** include *legitimate*, *reward*, and *coercive* types of positional power; and *expert* and *referent* (charisma) types of personal power. The model suggests that using personal power is more effective, specifically using expert power (becoming an expert at what you do).

Another leadership style, **transactional leadership**, assumes that people are motivated by rewards for accomplishments. This approach focuses on designing tasks and reward structures. In the transaction, the organization pays team members to complete a task or job. The leader penalizes those whose work does not meet an appropriate standard. This approach is used in most organizations to get things done, even though it does not focus on the human aspects of leadership, such as developing relationships.

Situational Leadership

When managing individuals and teams, leaders must incorporate **situational leadership**: the ability to adapt their leadership style to the needs of the individual, team, or organization. Situational leadership is based on the **Hersey-Blanchard model**. In their 1969 work *Management of Organizational Behavior*, Kenneth Blanchard and Paul Hersey recognized that all individuals are different, and the leader's message must be tailored to the situation.

Situational leadership acknowledges four types of leadership styles: directing, coaching, supporting, and delegating. The goal of situational leadership is to move subordinates through the different leadership styles, enabling them to delegate on their own and complete tasks relatively independently. This model focuses on the employee, rather than the leader. Each leadership style is measured by competency and commitment of the employees themselves.

An employee who needs to be managed by **directing** is typically new to their role or the organization. They are not yet knowledgeable about their role, so the manager focuses on giving clear direction and developing that person's skill level. These individuals are usually highly committed and excited about their new tasks, so during this stage, the manager should also focus on positive feedback.

When the **coaching** style is used, the employee has begun to develop their skill set, though training and guidance are still needed. At this point, the

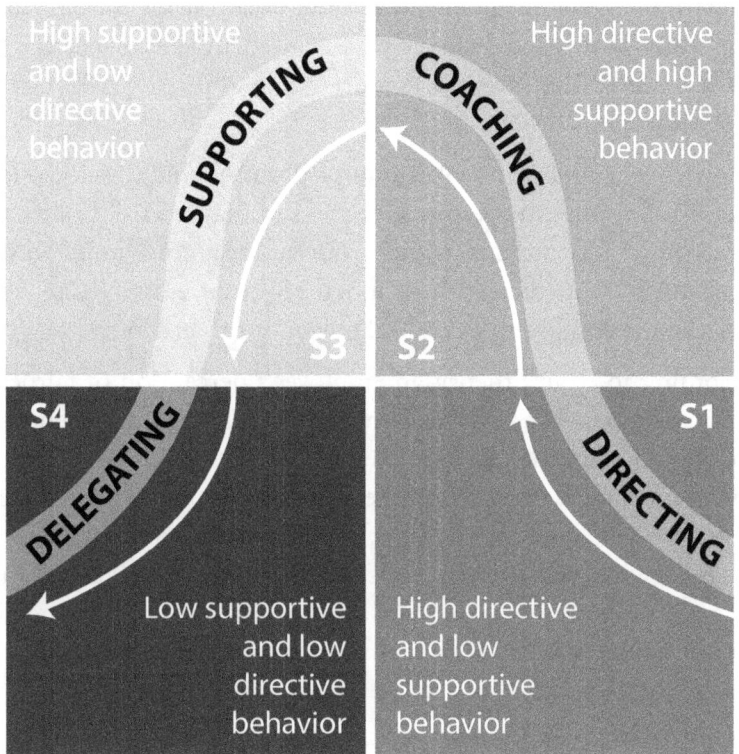

Figure 2.1. Situational Leadership

manager might do more suggesting and less telling. They will focus more on motivating and building relationships to ensure the employee's commitment.

The **supporting** style is used with an employee who may be competent but, through performance issues or other factors, is not fully committed to the role or organization. At this point, the leader moves away from giving instruction or focusing on tasks and instead puts time and effort into engaging and motivating.

When a leader is able to employ the **delegating** style, their subordinates feel empowered and that they have the competencies needed to perform their roles. The manager can now safely delegate tasks knowing they will be done effectively and in a timely manner.

People Management

In people management, a manager must understand both the people they are leading and their own styles and behaviors. **Emotional intelligence** is a person's ability to identify their own emotions and the emotions of others. Emotional intelligence allows a leader to adapt their style to a situation.

Leaders may use rewards to manage people. These rewards can be positive, such as recognition or a bonus, or they can be negative, such as discipline or loss of pay. In 1964, Victor H. Vroom developed the idea of **expectancy theory**, which states that individuals are motivated by their perceived expected outcome. That is, if an individual thinks there will be a positive reward, they are more likely to perform. The reverse of this can be true: If an employee believes there will be no reward or even punishment, their effort may be minimal or substandard.

HELPFUL HINT

Leadership cannot be executed in the same way for all individuals or circumstances. A strong leader recognizes this and adjusts accordingly.

A manager must strategically use rewards to encourage the desired behaviors. Building relationships and dialogue with team members creates an understanding of their needs. The manager can design appropriate positive rewards and limit the use of punishment.

Another management tool is **equity theory**, which focuses not only on the reward but also on the perceived fairness of that reward. Equity theory was developed by John S. Adams in the 1960s and examines how job satisfaction relates to rewards. It looks at how much effort an employee puts into a job compared to the employee's perceived reward for that effort.

According to equity theory, an employee's perception of fairness impacts their job performance and satisfaction. They will assess their talents and efforts and compare them to the talents and efforts of other employees. If an employee feels that their value is higher than their coworkers, they expect higher rewards. If not, they may change their level of effort or input to match what they now perceive is the appropriate reward. This perception may be accurate or inaccurate. A manager's responsibility is to create a sense of fairness for this individual. This may include a raise or additional income if warranted, or it may involve coaching.

Other Leadership Styles

There are other leadership styles outside the frameworks previously mentioned, but they are still relevant in the workplace.

In **bureaucratic leadership**, leaders follow rules closely and expect the same of their team members. This style is effective when working in dangerous conditions (e.g., operating heavy machinery, working with hazardous substances), when working directly with money, or when performing routine tasks. This style is much less effective in teams that require flexibility, creativity, or innovation.

A **charismatic leadership** style seeks to inspire and motivate team members. However, leaders who rely on charisma often focus on themselves and their own ambitions rather than the organization as a whole. Charismatic leaders may seem infallible, which can damage the organization if significant, inappropriate decisions are made.

A **servant leader** leads by meeting the needs of the team. Servant leaders lead by example and with integrity; they often show great generosity. This approach can foster a positive culture and high morale. Servant leadership requires time and dedication and may not be compatible with more authoritarian, rigid types of leadership.

Transformational leaders expect individuals to meet their potential; they also take personal responsibility for their own actions. Transformational leaders are inspirational; they set clear goals and are able to resolve conflict. This form of leadership encourages high productivity and engagement. According to researcher Bernard M. Bass, they gain the trust, respect, and admiration of others.

Clearly, leadership is not a "one size fits all" concept; instead, leaders must adapt their approach to fit a particular situation. It is important for leaders to develop a thorough understanding of various leadership frameworks and styles in order to adapt to changing situations.

EXAMPLES

1. Leadership theories that look at the personal characteristics of a leader are
   A) trait theories.
   B) situational theories.
   C) behavioral theories.
   D) contingency theories.

2. What is a primary dimension of behavioral theories of leadership?
   A) common sense in the workplace
   B) consideration of employees
   C) self-confidence and assertiveness
   D) task-relevant knowledge

Relationship Management

Effective communication requires building relationships. This means knowing and acknowledging the members of a team and building connections with candidates, vendors, other departments, and even the executive team. The ability to build and manage relationships is a critical skill for effective leaders.

Interpersonal skills are as important to leadership as the ability to inspire people. Relationships should be strategically managed through clear communication, active listening, responsiveness, and showing interest in others. Relationship management builds loyalty, trust, and a culture of increased productivity, engagement, and tenure.

In the digital age, multiple avenues of communication are used to establish relationships. Knowing the audience and their preferred methods can go a long way toward enhancing communication. Going beyond the traditional meeting or phone call, leaders should consider how emails, texting, the internet, the intranet, and social media can build relationships.

Networking is one way to build relationships; it may occur within an organization, community, or profession. **Networking** establishes a mutually beneficial affiliation with other employees, clients, vendors, or organizations. Networking can be done in a casual setting, for example, in conference lunches where people share who they are and what they do. Networking can also take place in a more formal setting through association meetings or management training programs. Finally, networking increasingly takes place online via social media and webinars.

Networking is more than just informing others about your product or service. Through networking, employees gain additional knowledge, learn best practices, tap into problem-solving resources, and build successful teams.

Offering new hires mentoring opportunities can frontload their networking in an organization, opening up resources and collaboration to help them do their jobs effectively.

Relationship building happens when two or more people connect and associate. Relationship building at work is critical because it creates opportunity for coaching, collaboration, and idea sharing. When building a relationship, it is important to establish trust and to respect the psychological contract (explained below).

In order to build trust, both parties must be authentic, develop mutual respect, and create a meaningful connection. Trust is built over time as each party adheres to the unwritten set of rules that govern their interactions. These rules are called the **psychological contract** and refer to a set of expectations that are established between two parties (e.g., employers, managers, employees, or coworkers). Clear and effective communication can positively impact a psychological contract that is dynamic and changes over time.

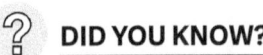

DID YOU KNOW?

The concept of the psychological contract was developed by organizational scholar Denise Rousseau in her 1989 article "Psychological and Implied Contracts in Organizations."

Breaking a psychological contract can lead to disengagement and turnover as the parties experience a loss of trust.

Teamwork happens when various people throughout a department, organization, or community come together to work on a single goal. This may involve creating, problem-solving, or advising. Often, teamwork results in a rewarding outcome since it brings together a diverse group of ideas, skills, and abilities.

Psychologist Bruce Tuckman created a model outlining the development sequence of a group. He concluded that there are four phases every group must undergo to become successful: forming, storming, norming, and performing. Team leaders can guide individuals through these stages so they can complete them in a timely manner.

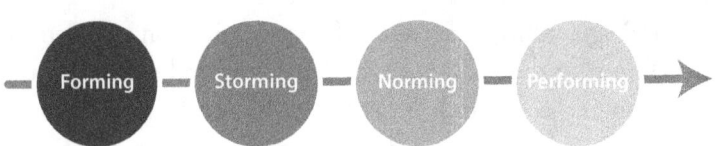

Figure 2.2. Development Sequence of a Group

Forming happens when a group first comes together. Individuals are polite, and all of the rules are not fully understood. Forming is followed by **storming**, where participants start to push boundaries and conflict develops. This is normal, and groups should not only expect but also embrace this stage since it allows them to establish processes, roles, and rules. Likewise it allows the team to move into **norming**, where they come together as a unit, resolve their differences, and create stronger relationships. In the final stage, **performing**, the team can work with the least amount of friction as processes have been established.

Conflict Management and Resolution

Human resources must support the organization and individuals in conflict management and resolution. Ignoring conflicts can lead to distrust, lowered engagement and productivity, and higher turnover. Unfortunately, many people choose to avoid conflict because they are uncomfortable or they do not know how to solve the conflict on their own. A human resources professional can mediate and participate in conflict resolution. HR also trains employees and supervisors to reduce conflict.

It is important to understand that conflict is not only natural; it is to be expected. An organization must recognize this so that employees can resolve conflict in a safe and supportive manner. Conflict has many root causes. Understanding these causes and taking the time to determine them is a necessary part of resolving and reducing conflict. **Conflict resolution** involves exploring the underlying reasons for disagreement and lack of alignment among teams and individuals.

When resolving conflict, the involved employees should come together to discuss the issues. Some simple guidelines for starting this conversation include setting the ground rules, allowing each person an opportunity to share, encouraging active listening and paraphrasing, and brainstorming mutually agreeable solutions.

Sometimes outside resources are needed. For example, legal counsel is advisable when dealing with conflict that is severe or that could lead to liability issues (e.g., harassment or discrimination).

Organizational conflict describes the natural conflict or disagreement that develops between employees, departments, or functions. There are three basic sources of conflict: relationship, task, and process.

1. **Relationship conflict** involves interpersonal issues between individuals and affects how employees work together and the social issues surrounding interactions.
2. **Task conflict** arises when parties disagree about the content or outcome of tasks, procedures, or goals. Task conflict focuses on "what" should be done.
3. **Process conflict** involves disagreement over "how" the team should complete certain tasks.

Conflict can happen on a micro level between two people or on a macro level between two organizations. **Intra-organizational conflict** is between individuals, departments, or functions within the same company. **Inter-organizational conflict** involves multiple companies or organizations. Conflicts between customers and vendors or among competitors are inter-organizational conflicts.

There are several styles of conflict resolution and negation. It is important to understand all the styles because a particular situation may require one or more styles to resolve the issue. These styles include competing, accommodating, avoiding, compromising, and collaborating.

- In **competing**, each side pursues their own interests, focusing on short-term gains. A person will use competing when they need to act quickly, or when there is no room to negotiate.
- In **accommodating**, one side wins and the other loses. Accommodating is used when maintaining relationships and goodwill is a priority.
- In **avoiding**, both sides lose. This style is often used by two individuals who want to avoid conflict. It can be a way of getting revenge or being passive-aggressive.
- In **compromising**, both parties win a little and lose a little. Often mistaken for collaboration, compromising is more about meeting in the middle than determining a mutually beneficial outcome.
- **Collaborating** creates a win-win outcome. This style focuses on meeting both parties' needs and arriving at mutually beneficial solutions.

As human resources professionals are asked to be involved in conflict resolution, helping the parties move toward collaboration leads to positive outcomes that each side can agree on.

Negotiation

Many of the principles used in conflict resolution apply to negotiation. The key difference is that conflict resolution focuses on an issue or problem that needs to be solved, whereas in **negotiation** two parties share an objective. Human resources professionals use negotiation in many different areas including employment offers, union contacts, benefit purchasing, and dispute resolution.

DID YOU KNOW?

Roger Fisher, William Ury, and Bruce Patton developed the concept of principled negotiation in their 1991 work *Getting to Yes: Negotiating Agreement Without Giving In*.

The negotiation process creates an agreement between two or more parties. These can be formal agreements or verbal agreements. It is important to know when these agreements are legally binding and approach negotiations appropriately.

An important step in negotiation is **perspective-taking**: understanding the other person's point of view. A good negotiator helps the other party understand their point of view by speaking clearly about their needs, using data and information to support their position, or creating a story or narrative around their perspective. It is also important to take time to understand the other person. That allows a negotiator to improve their position and know where their needs are in regard to the situation.

Principled bargaining, or principled negotiation, happens when both sides focus on objective outcomes, eliminating emotional disagreements or grandstanding. Elements of principled bargaining include separating the emotions from the problem, focusing on interests rather than positions, looking for options that include mutual gains, and using objective criteria.

Another negotiation tactic is auction. In an **auction**, buyers compete against one another for an item or outcome. The competitive nature of auction may drive the price higher if the outcome, such as a sale of a business, is in high demand.

However, it may also lead to decisions based solely on monetary gain rather than on a win-win for everyone involved.

Interest-based bargaining, like principled bargaining, recognizes the importance of both parties and works toward the win-win outcome. This type of bargaining, unlike auction, keeps the relationships intact, avoiding a "win at all cost" mentality. This is in contrast to position-based bargaining in which there are winners and losers. **Position-based bargaining** is a competition that pits the sides against each other and can often breed resentment.

As organizations use negotiation techniques for labor and employee relations, it is critical that relationship management and teamwork are recognized as key influences. It is important to choose the negotiation tactic that will maintain employee trust and engagement even after the negotiations are completed.

EXAMPLE

3. Which form of conflict resolution focuses on meeting the needs of both parties?
    - **A)** accommodating
    - **B)** avoiding
    - **C)** compromising
    - **D)** collaborating

Communication

Communication is an important aspect of trust, healthy relationships, conflict resolution, and negotiation. Understanding the basics of communication helps teams and departments to collaborate effectively.

Aspects of Communication

Communication can be broken down into different components. The **source** or **sender** is the individual or team that created the original message. This person can communicate the message in different ways and use their communication skills to create the message. It may be verbal, written, nonverbal, or electronic. The **message** itself is the content or idea that the sender is communicating.

The **receiver** is the person or audience that receives and interprets the message. It is important to note that the receiver's own experiences, skills, and abilities will impact how they receive and interpret the message. The sender should create the message with the receiver in mind. The human resources department must often assess the receiver's biases when creating global messages to ensure clarity and relevance within a communication.

Active listening happens when the receiver fully focuses on the message, not allowing outer or internal distractions. During active listening, the receiver should give **message feedback** through nonverbal cues like nodding or smiling, or through paraphrasing or asking clarifying questions.

When giving feedback to an individual or a group, the manager must consider all elements of communication. In particular, managers should ask themselves, "Who is the receiver of the feedback and how will they receive the message I am trying to send?" Managers must be transparent with feedback even if it makes the sender uncomfortable. An employee must receive feedback and understand expectations so they can modify or continue behaviors.

One feedback tool is the **SBI model** developed by the Center for Creative Leadership. This model describes the situation (S), then the behavior (B), and finally the impact (I) or reaction to the behavior. The SBI model shifts the focus from the individual to the actual behavior, creating a coaching opportunity.

Employee Communications

An organization uses employee communications to share knowledge with and get feedback from employees. The medium, manner, tone, and frequency of communications affect employee motivation and organizational success. People need regular and open access to information, to ask questions, and to provide feedback. Then they can align themselves with the goals, strategies, and objectives of the organization, department, or team.

Employee communications can be organization-wide (macro level) or employee-specific (micro level). They can take many forms, including:

- announcement of a new product or service
- information about company-wide benefits and open enrollment
- disclosure of company quarterly earnings
- announcement of business changes
- formal and informal feedback
- invitation to company-wide events
- explanation of new processes

Using a combination of media to convey information is a good way to reach employees in different locations, who have different schedules, and who have different learning styles. Below are some examples of **media** used:

- email messages
- bulletin boards
- company intranet
- company newsletters
- company-wide halls
- team or department meetings
- conference calls
- one-on-one conversations
- training sessions
- social media

The messages should be tailored to the type of **communications media** as well as to the receiver (i.e., the whole company or a specific group of employees). Open lines maintain transparency with employees and ensure that messages are conveyed to and understood by them. It is essential that information can flow upward from employees to leadership for free exchange between both sides.

A company and its employees can benefit from effective employee communications in many ways:

- Roles in the organization are clarified, and employees recognize how they contribute to the "bottom line" or mission.
- Employees better understand changes in the organization by asking questions and absorbing information to adapt to those changes. This reduces anxiety, which would lead to lower productivity or higher turnover.
- Customer service improves when employees fully appreciate the product or service and understand what is expected of them.
- Leadership can gain valuable input from staff about products and services, operations, or other issues, helping them to advance the organization's mission.
- Consistent and open communication establishes trust and encourages loyalty to the organization. Being upfront and honest can dispel rumors and encourage employees to ask questions.

Leadership should communicate information regularly to staff and solicit feedback. Furthermore, leadership must be responsive to feedback. Two-way communication will maintain a dialogue, reinforce trust, and generate new ideas. Companies undergoing change should establish a communications plan to ensure that messages are fully understood.

When creating a new product, process, policy, or program, focus groups can be a good source of ideas, input, and knowledge. A **focus group** is a small group of people whose response to a product or idea is considered representative of the larger population. A focus group's goal must be clearly defined before it meets. Additionally, a trained facilitator must walk the team through predetermined exercises and questions that will allow it to be productive. Conversations are facilitated through open-ended questions. Often there is a separate recorder so that the facilitator is not distracted by taking notes.

Another type of group or team collaboration is a **staff** or **team meeting**. These meetings should also have a recorder to ensure ideas are captured, action items are noted, and specific roles are assigned. When leading this type of meeting, creating and following an agenda can encourage productivity.

EXAMPLE

4. In active listening, the listener

　A) interrupts the speaker to show they understand the speaker's message.

　B) actively acknowledges the speaker by taking notes and focusing on a notepad.

　C) should nod, make eye contact, and paraphrase the speaker at the end of the talk.

　D) must give verbal feedback as the speaker talks to show they are listening.

Global and Cultural Effectiveness

> **HELPFUL HINT**
>
> P. Christopher Earley and Elaine Mosakowski elaborated on the concept of cultural intelligence in the October 2004 issue of the *Harvard Business Review*.

Most organizations operate within the global economy. Those that do not must still acknowledge multiple cultures and diversity within their workplace. **Cultural intelligence (CQ)** is an outsider's ability to understand the unfamiliar aspects of a different culture and even blend in. There are a number of models that help employers understand cultural diversity on both a global and organizational level.

Operating in a Diverse Workplace

According to anthropologist Edward T. Hall, cultures are characterized by high and low contexts. In a high-context culture numerous rules are understood but not defined. A **high-context culture** can be confusing for someone who is unfamiliar with the many unwritten rules that are understood. Norms may not be clearly articulated, people may rely more on body language, and emotions may not be expressed openly. On the other hand, a **low-context culture** has clear rules that are more easily communicated to newcomers, eliminating confusion early on. People may be more outspoken and expressive, with more emphasis on spoken communication than body language.

Social psychologist Geert Hofstede developed a **cultural dimensions theory** that organizations use to understand cultures and perform globally. Hofstede's model is based on six cultural dimensions:

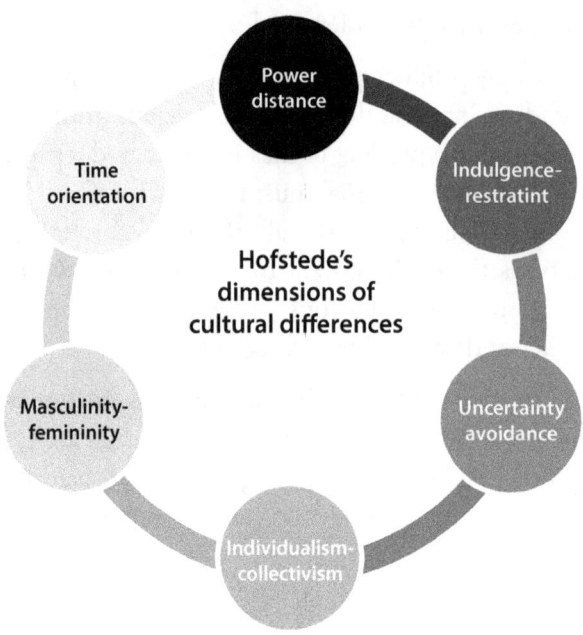

Figure 2.3. Hofstede's Cultural Dimensions Theory

1. The **power distance index** refers to the extent that inequality in power is accepted.
2. **Individualism versus collectivism**, or to what degree individuals are reliant on or obligated to others.

3. **Uncertainty avoidance**, meaning to what extent uncertainty and risk are accepted.

4. **Masculinity versus femininity**, or attitude toward gender equality (a "masculine culture" features distinct gender roles, whereas a "feminine culture" has fluid gender roles).

5. **Short-term versus long-term orientation**, or how much a culture views future rewards versus present gratification.

6. **Indulgence versus restraint**, or the degree to which a culture controls or regulates gratification.

A similar cultural model is **Trompenaars cultural dimensions** model. Dutch author Fons Trompenaars developed these seven cultural dimensions:

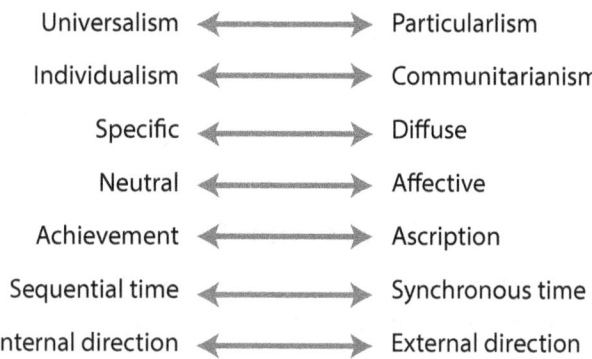

Figure 2.4. Trompenaars Cultural Dimensions

1. **Universalism versus particularism**: Universalism focuses on consistent rules for all, whereas particularism focuses on relationships and embraces decisions based on nepotism.

2. **Individualism versus communitarianism**: In individualism the outcomes of one's life are based on one's actions; in communitarianism people succeed or fail as a group.

3. **Specific versus diffuse**: In a specific culture work and home are kept separate; in a diffuse culture these two parts of life are interconnected.

4. **Neutral versus affective**: In a neutral culture people conceal their emotions, whereas in an affective culture people are emotionally demonstrative, even in the workplace.

5. **Achievement versus ascription**: In an achievement culture individuals gain status through knowledge and skills; in an ascription culture individuals have status based on predetermined position or connections.

6. **Sequential time versus synchronous time**: In a sequential culture time is literal, and punctuality is very important; in a synchronous culture time is flexible, and punctuality is less important.

7. **Internal direction versus external direction**: In a culture based on internal direction, individuals believe they can control their

environment, whereas people in a culture based on external direction believe they work with the environment they are given.

Management professor Edgar Schein developed another model of organizational culture. Schein's model contends that an organization's values shape its practices and behaviors. That is, culture is not created quickly but rather over time as different practices are put into place.

Schein's model has three levels of organizational culture: artifacts, values, and basic assumptions.

1. An organization's cultural **artifacts** are the visible part of the culture that can be seen by an outsider. They may include actual physical items such as trophies, office design, or pictures. Artifacts may also be invisible items like language, stories, and traditions.
2. The organization's **values** are a shared understanding of how business will be done.
3. Basic **assumptions** are shared ideas among individuals, such as how space is used, what is moral, or what is ethical.

Operating in a Global Environment

Companies with locations around the world must balance their culture with the cultures of different countries and regions. Communication in multiple languages and time zones can be a challenge. It is critical to create communication programs and strategies to account for a diverse and changing workforce.

Organizations can take additional steps, such as providing language and cultural classes. Not only do these give employees additional skill sets; they also eliminate unconscious biases and raise awareness about diversity. Cultural awareness and training, beyond language classes, should be incorporated into the fabric of the company. All employees should be exposed to this type of training on a regular basis.

Several human resource information systems (HRIS), learning management systems (LMS), payroll, and communication platforms operate on a global level. Picking the right one allows the organization to roll out global programs where employees around the world have access to the same information. Still, HR responsibilities differ among countries, especially when it comes to payroll and benefits.

Expatriates—employees living outside their home countries—require preparation and training before their assignment begins. Regular check-ins on performance and progress should take place over the course of the assignment. And when they return to their home country, a clear career path should be determined.

Recruitment, selection, and onboarding should be addressed on a global level to enhance company-wide collaboration. Not only does the organization need to understand local laws and other workplace norms; items such as negotiating salary may be dictated by the government or trade unions also. Additionally, HR and management should consider whether to hire local talent instead of moving people from other locations. Benefits may be different, and expectations may be dictated by laws or rules. Legal compliance must be a top priority when conducting business globally.

Advocating for a Diverse and Inclusive Workplace

Most successful organizations understand that diversity within the workforce leads to higher creativity and profitability. Still, a more diverse workforce can mean differences in perceptions and expectations based on experiences, norms, and attitudes.

The human resources team is the heart of cultural and diversity integration. HR provides opportunity for open dialogue and training in inclusion and equity. An inclusive work environment not only promotes a diverse membership; it also ensures welcoming behaviors and social norms. An inclusive environment encourages access, choice, opportunity, and policies that incorporate and support all employees.

Equity promotes fairness by providing support and resources to individuals to allow them to reach their full potential. It also focuses on **removal of barriers** that prohibit specific classes of people from succeeding. This may be as simple as allowing a flexible schedule to accommodate parents with childcare needs. It may also include translating documents so employees can read communications in their first languages. It is important that all employees are able to **assimilate** into the organization's culture, but assimilation also requires that culture to be open and welcoming.

Training in sensitivity and unconscious biases can have a positive impact on inclusion. An **unconscious bias** is an unintentional stereotype or perception a person has. Unconscious biases can adversely affect the workplace if not addressed. It is important that individuals recognize any actions they take or words they use that might alienate other people. Addressing unconscious biases may be done in a group setting or one-on-one.

When creating an inclusive environment, it is important to involve the workforce, solicit feedback, and embrace disagreement. HR should create opportunities for relationship building and dialogue. This may be done in social settings or formal meetings.

EXAMPLE

5. Which of the following HR responsibilities is most likely to differ from country to country?
    - **A)** job analysis
    - **B)** training and development
    - **C)** compensation and benefits
    - **D)** personnel records

Answer Key

1. **A)** Trait theories maintain that effective leaders share several common traits, beliefs, and thought processes.

2. **B)** Behavioral theories focus on how leaders act toward others.

3. **D)** Collaborating focuses on meeting both parties' needs while looking for mutually beneficial solutions.

4. **C)** Active listening means being engaged with the speaker and demonstrating that engagement through message cues like body language (eye contact, nodding, facing the speaker) and paraphrasing the speaker's words at the appropriate time to show they understand the message.

5. **C)** HR responsibilities differ among countries, especially when it comes to compensation and benefits.

3 Workforce Planning and Management

Equal Employment Opportunity

The doctrine of **Equal Employment Opportunity** prohibits discrimination against applicants and employees due to certain personal characteristics like race, color, sex, and other protected classifications. This doctrine ensures fair treatment in finding work, being paid, getting promoted, and opportunities for professional development.

The Equal Employment Opportunity Commission

The **US Equal Employment Opportunity Commission (EEOC)** enforces federal laws prohibiting employment discrimination. The EEOC is an independent federal agency.

TABLE 3.1. Federal Laws Prohibiting Discrimination in Employment

FEDERAL LAW	PROTECTIONS
Title VII of the Civil Rights Act of 1964	Prohibits employment discrimination on the basis of race, color, religion, national origin, or sex. Employers must reasonably accommodate applicants' and employees' sincerely held religious practices, unless doing so would impose an undue hardship on the business. In 2020, the Supreme Court affirmed that gay and transgender people are protected in the workplace under this law on the basis of sex.
Pregnancy Discrimination Act (PDA)	Amends Title VII to prohibit discrimination against a woman because of pregnancy, childbirth, or a medical condition related to pregnancy or childbirth.
Equal Pay Act of 1963	Makes it illegal to pay different wages to men and women if they perform equal work in the same workplace.
Age Discrimination in Employment Act of 1967 (ADEA)	Prohibits discrimination against applicants or employees based on age (those forty or older).

TABLE 3.1. Federal Laws Prohibiting Discrimination in Employment (continued)

FEDERAL LAW	PROTECTIONS
Title I of the Americans with Disabilities Act of 1990 (ADA)	Prohibits employment discrimination against qualified people who have a disability. Employers must reasonably accommodate the physical or mental limitations of an otherwise qualified applicant or employee with a disability, unless doing so would impose an undue hardship on the business. The Rehabilitation Act of 1973 prohibits discrimination against qualified employees or applicants with disabilities in the federal government.
Genetic Information Nondiscrimination Act of 2008 (GINA)	Prohibits discrimination against employees or applicants because of genetic information. Genetic information includes information about an individual's genetic tests, the genetic tests of their family members, or their family medical history.

According to the laws listed in Table 3.1, federal law forbids discrimination in every aspect of employment, including hiring, compensation, discipline, and termination. It is also illegal to retaliate against a person because they reported discrimination, filed a charge of discrimination, or participated in an employment discrimination investigation or lawsuit. Employers must post notices describing the federal laws prohibiting job discrimination based on race, color, religion, sex (including pregnancy), national origin, age (forty or older), disability, or genetic information.

Not all federal laws apply to all employers. Employers with fewer than a certain number of employees may not be subject to nondiscrimination laws.

TABLE 3.2. Small Businesses and Federal Discrimination Laws

SIZE OF BUSINESS	WHAT FEDERAL LAWS APPLY
Business with at least 1 employee	Equal Pay Act of 1963
Business with 15–19 employees	Equal Pay Act of 1963 Title VII of the Civil Rights Act of 1964 Pregnancy Discrimination Act (PDA) Title I of the Americans with Disabilities Act of 1990 (ADA) Genetic Information Nondiscrimination Act of 2008 (GINA)
Business with 20 or more employees	Equal Pay Act of 1963 Title VII of the Civil Rights Act of 1964 Pregnancy Discrimination Act (PDA) Title I of the Americans with Disabilities Act of 1990 (ADA) Genetic Information Nondiscrimination Act of 2008 (GINA) Age Discrimination in Employment Act of 1967 (ADEA)

Additionally, some states and localities have enacted their own nondiscrimination laws that certain employers must follow. Employers should monitor employment laws in all states they operate in and determine what laws apply.

Federal EEO laws also prohibit an employer from using employment policies and practices that have a disproportionately negative effect on applicants or employees of a protected class if the policies or practices at issue are not job-related and necessary to the business's operation. The laws also prohibit an employer from using employment policies and practices that have a disproportionately negative impact on applicants or employees forty or older if the policies or practices are not based on a reasonable factor other than age. These adverse effects on protected classes are called disparate treatment or disparate impact.

Both disparate impact and disparate treatment refer to discrimination. They differ when it comes to intention. **Disparate treatment** is *intentional* bias against a protected class. Examples of disparate treatment include a policy against hiring someone who is pregnant or only promoting individuals of a certain race.

Disparate impact occurs when a process or procedure is designed in a way that is discriminatory against a certain protected class. Such policies may appear neutral, but they create a discriminatory outcome. Examples include requiring an individual to own a car even if it is not necessary for the job, or expecting employees to live in a certain area.

Figure 3.1. Disparate Treatment

Figure 3.2. Disparate Impact

WORKFORCE PLANNING AND MANAGEMENT

Precedent for disparate impact was established in the 1971 Supreme Court ruling in *Griggs v. Duke Power Co.* In ***Griggs v. Duke Power Co.***, the Supreme Court ruled that the employer has the burden of showing that any selection process is job related and that lack of intent does not make the practice lawful if it inadvertently causes discrimination based on a protected class.

What Employers May Not Do

To comply with federal law and to provide equal opportunity to all employees and applicants, employers may NOT do certain things in their employment practices. Prohibited acts are based on race, color, religion, sex (including pregnancy, sexual orientation, or gender identity), national origin, age (forty or older), disability, or genetic information. Prohibited acts include:

- advertising a job that shows a preference based on a protected class
- recruiting new employees in a way that results in discrimination based on a protected class
- discriminating against an applicant or refusing to give an application to a person of a certain protected class
- requiring preemployment or post-employment examinations that may be inherently discriminatory
- considering a person's characteristic (protected class) when making decisions about job referrals
- making decisions about job assignments or promotions based on an employee's protected class
- discriminating in the way employees are paid, based on protected class
- considering an employee's protected class when taking a disciplinary action
- refusing a reasonable accommodation to a disabled employee, unless doing so would cause an undue hardship to business operations
- refusing to accommodate an individual's sincerely held religious beliefs and attendance at religious services, unless doing so would cause a substantial burden to the business

Reasonable accommodations are changes or adjustments that do not create an undue hardship for an organization. These might include job restructuring, schedule changes, or flexibility in hours. Reasonable accommodations may also include tools or aids that help an employee complete a job. Personal items like medications, hearing aids, or wheelchairs are not reasonable accommodations.

Undue hardship is determined on a case-by-case basis based on each company's situation. One key of reasonable accommodations is knowing the role's essential job functions and then determining what accommodations can be made so the person can perform these job responsibilities.

Harassment

The same laws that prohibit discrimination also prohibit harassment based on protected class. **Harassment** and bullying can take the form of slurs, graffiti,

> **HELPFUL HINT**
>
> Disparate treatment was established by the *McDonnell Douglas Corp. v. Green* case in 1973.

offensive or derogatory comments, or other verbal or physical conduct. It is also illegal to harass someone because they have complained about discrimination, filed a charge of discrimination, or participated in an employment discrimination investigation or lawsuit.

Bullying is harassing conduct that creates an intimidating or offensive work environment with enough frequency or severity that this conduct would affect a reasonable person's performance. Bullying behavior can include rudeness, sarcasm, or hostility if it is intended to interfere with the victim's ability to perform their duties. **Illegal harassment** is when this behavior is based or targeted on an individual being part of a protected class.

Sexual harassment is a specific type of harassment that includes unwelcome sexual advances, requests for sexual favors, and other sexual conduct. Any conduct of a sexual nature that makes an employee uncomfortable has the potential to be sexual harassment. The harasser can be the victim's supervisor, a supervisor in another area, a coworker, or someone who is not an employee, like a client or customer.

Harassment outside of the workplace may also be illegal if there is a link with the workplace. For example, a supervisor who harasses an employee while driving them to a meeting may be breaking the law. For these reasons, organizations typically develop strict policies against harassment with detailed procedures to report, investigate, and handle complaints.

Sexual harassment can take two main forms: quid pro quo or hostile work environment. **Quid pro quo**, (Latin for "this for that") occurs when certain employment outcomes are linked to sexual favors. This could be a job offer, promotion, raise, or other similar employment decision.

A **hostile work environment** is one in which intimidating or offensive working conditions impact an individual's ability to work or perform their job. The law does not forbid mild misconduct like teasing, occasional comments, or some minor isolated incidents. But harassment becomes illegal if it is so pervasive or severe that it creates a hostile or offensive work environment, or if it results in an adverse employment decision, such as termination or demotion of a victim.

Several court cases have defined sexual harassment in the workplace. In 1986, the Supreme Court decided *Meritor Savings Bank v. Vinson*. This was the first case in which courts recognized a hostile work environment as discrimination under Title VII.

In *Meritor Savings Bank v. Vinson*, a bank teller named Mechelle Vinson was repeatedly sexually assaulted and humiliated by her supervisor. She was eventually fired, ostensibly for misusing sick time. Vinson said her supervisor coerced her into sexual relations and created a hostile work environment. In a unanimous decision, the Court found that a hostile work environment characterized by sexually inappropriate conditions was a form of discrimination based on sex under the Civil Rights Act of 1964.

In 1998, two landmark cases further defined sexual harassment. In ***Burlington Industries, Inc., v. Ellerth***, Kimberly Ellerth accused her supervisor of sexual harassment, quit her job, and sued the company. She claimed her supervisor threatened her with retaliation if she did not engage in a sexual relationship with him. Even though Burlington Industries had a sexual harassment policy, Ellerth did not complain because she would have had to report the misconduct she endured to her harasser. The Court found that even though Ellerth had suffered no tangible adverse job consequences, Burlington Industries was still liable for the hostile work environment.

In *Faragher v. City of Boca Raton*, Florida lifeguard Beth Ann Faragher accused two male supervisors of making offensive remarks and inappropriate touching, which created a hostile work environment. Faragher did not immediately complain, but the Supreme Court still found the City of Boca Raton liable for the supervisors' misconduct.

The outcome of *Ellerth* and *Faragher* was that, even if an employer is unaware of harassment, the organization is still liable when harassment is perpetrated by a supervisor. The company may have an affirmative defense only if it shows it took reasonable care to prevent or correct harassment promptly, and if the employee failed to report the incident through channels provided by the employer.

Retaliation is taking an adverse action against an employee or applicant because they complain about harassment, raise concerns about violations, or engage in other protected behavior. It is illegal to retaliate against an individual for raising a legitimate harassment complaint or concern. An organization should have policies and training around retaliation to ensure that those who register a complaint are protected.

The 2016 Supreme Court case **Green v. Brennan** found that the filing period for an aggrieved employee to file a workplace discrimination complaint begins once they give notice of resignation, not at the date of resignation.

Constructive Discharge/Forced Resignation

Another discriminatory practice under federal law is when an employer forces an employee to resign or makes the work environment so intolerable that a reasonable person could not sustain employment. This is called constructive discharge. In **constructive discharge**, the work environment is unbearable to the point that an employee of a protected class feels they have no other choice than to quit their job. Usually such an environment involves sexual harassment or discrimination.

Bona Fide Occupational Qualification

A **bona fide occupational qualification (BFOQ)** is a legitimate reason to exclude a person based on a protected class that would otherwise be illegal. The courts define the legal use of BFOQ very narrowly, and it must directly relate to the ability to perform the job. An example is requiring an employee to stand for a certain period of time due to a piece of equipment that cannot be changed or modified.

Dress Code

Under the law, employers may establish dress codes. Dress codes might apply to all employees or to employees within certain job categories. There are some exceptions.

Some dress codes might conflict with certain religious beliefs or practices. But a dress code may not punish employees because of their national origin. For example, an employer may not prohibit certain traditional or culturally significant attire while allowing casual attire. In addition, if the dress code conflicts with an employee's religious practices and the employee requests an accommodation, the employer must make an exception or modification to the dress code unless doing so would result in undue hardship. (The same rule applies to employees with disabilities who request a reasonable accommodation.)

Equal Employment Opportunity Complaints

If an employee or job applicant believes they have experienced discrimination at work, they can file a **charge of discrimination**, or Equal Employment Opportunity (EEO) complaint.

Filing an EEO complaint does not automatically mean the company has committed any wrongdoing. Rather, a **charge of discrimination** is a formal allegation that an employer has discriminated against the complainant. The EEOC must then investigate the situation and decide if there is reasonable cause to believe that discrimination has occurred. Furthermore, not every employee is protected by the EEOC. As addressed above in Table 3.2, some employers are exempt from certain federal laws.

Complainants must file a charge of discrimination with the EEOC before filing a job discrimination lawsuit against an employer. The only law enforced by the EEOC that does not require a charge of discrimination is the Equal Pay Act. There are also time limits for filing a charge of discrimination.

Employers must also adhere to EEO reporting requirements by keeping certain employment records. Furthermore, private sector employers with more than 100 employees must make workforce data available to the EEOC via an **EEO-1 Report**. The EEOC collects this data whether or not a charge has been filed against the company. Workforce data is used in law enforcement, employer self-assessment, and federal research. Although a company's specific data remains confidential, aggregated data is available to the public.

EXAMPLES

1. Which federal agency has the primary responsibility to enforce employment nondiscrimination laws?
    - A) Department of Labor
    - B) Equal Employment Opportunity Commission
    - C) Department of Homeland Security
    - D) Office of the Attorney General

2. Which of the following laws deals directly with pay discrimination?
   A) Fair Labor Standards Act
   B) affirmative action
   C) Patient Protection and Affordable Care Act (PPACA)
   D) Equal Pay Act

Affirmative Action Planning

Affirmative action is the policy of providing opportunities specifically for, and favoring members of, a disadvantaged minority group that has historically experienced discrimination. Affirmative action may include outreach to minority candidates, special training programs, and other positive steps to ensure a diverse workforce. Employers who are subject to affirmative action typically develop formalized affirmative action plans (AAP) and policies. These plans are reviewed annually. Companies maintain documentation to ensure compliance with federal rules and regulations.

Developing Affirmative Action Plans

An affirmative action plan (AAP) or program is a tool employers develop and use to achieve their affirmative action goals. AAPs measure and evaluate the composition of the workforce, or the demographic makeup of the organization, and compare it to the relative composition of the available labor pools, or those in the same geographic region. An AAP also ensures equal employment opportunity by embedding this philosophy into the organization's employment practices, employment decisions, compensation programs, and performance management systems. Furthermore, AAPs include the practical steps an organization will take when people of certain classifications are underutilized.

AAPs typically outline a goal-setting process that is used to target and measure the effectiveness of affirmative action efforts to prevent and eliminate discrimination. Employers typically audit and report on their affirmative action plans on an annual basis, measuring their progress. Employers are prohibited, however, from establishing racial quotas or engaging in preferential treatment of certain groups (including women and minorities). AAPs must be signed by a company officer and be made available to internal employees and vendors.

Affirmative Action Requirements for Government Contractors and the OFCCP

In the United States, under **Executive Order 11248, Section 503 of the Rehabilitation Act of 1973**, and **Section 4212 of the Vietnam Era Veterans' Readjustment Assistance Act**, government contractors and subcontractors must provide affirmative action when recruiting, hiring, and employing qualified minorities, women, people with disabilities, and covered veterans. These policies require federal contractors and subcontractors to take affirmative action to ensure that all individuals have an equal opportunity for employment, without regard to race, color, religion, sex, national origin, disability, or status as a Vietnam-era or special disabled veteran.

The US Department of Labor's **Office of Federal Contract Compliance Programs (OFCCP)** enforces affirmative action laws, regulations, and executive orders with government contractors. To maintain a contract with the federal government, the OFCCP requires a contractor to practice affirmative action and nondiscrimination in employment. The OFCCP routinely investigates contractors' employment practices and complaints of discrimination. Failure to comply with nondiscrimination or affirmative action provisions of federal law is a violation of the contract. A contractor found to be in violation may have its contracts terminated or suspended, and the contractor may be deemed ineligible for future government contracts.

Under **Executive Order 11246**, non-construction contractors with fifty or more employees and government contracts of $50,000 or more are required to develop and implement a written affirmative action plan (AAP). The plan is kept on file and carried out by the contractor, and it is submitted to the OFCCP upon the agency's request.

Like other AAPs, government contractors' AAPs identify utilization of women and minorities in the contractors' workforce. Underutilization occurs when fewer minorities or women occupy a particular job group than would reasonably be expected based on their availability. Availability is determined by the predominance of qualified women and minorities in the geographical location of the company or site. Based on analyses of the availability of qualified individuals, contractors must establish goals to reduce or overcome underutilization. Employers are expected to consider the candidacy of qualified women and minorities and to provide them with employment opportunities and advancement. However, employment decisions are to be made on a nondiscriminatory basis. Finally, according to federal regulations, the OFCCP may not penalize contractors for not meeting goals.

For contractors in the construction industry, the OFCCP has established a distinct approach to affirmative action due to the seasonal and temporary nature of the construction workforce. For these businesses, the OFCCP, rather than the contractor, assigns goals and affirmative action that must be undertaken. For example, in 1980 the industry developed the goal of employing women for 6.9 percent of construction labor hours; this goal is still in effect today. The regulations also specify the good faith steps construction contractors must take in order to increase the hiring of minorities and women.

EXAMPLES

3. Which of the following statements about affirmative action plans (AAPs) is true?

    A) All employers with over 100 employees are required to have an AAP.

    B) An AAP is required for employers who have been found to discriminate against employees.

C) An AAP is required by the Fair Labor Standards Act.

D) An AAP must be signed by a company officer and made available to internal employees and vendors.

4. What is the difference between affirmative action and Equal Employment Opportunity?

A) Equal Employment Opportunity is required by law in the United States.

B) Affirmative action applies to small businesses and private organizations.

C) Affirmative action is required of government contractors.

D) Equal Employment Opportunity sets quotas for hiring in businesses throughout the US.

Job Descriptions

Every position within an organization should have a corresponding **job description** that accurately and completely describes the activities of a job. The job description is a document that provides an overview of the position's major responsibilities and identifies the **knowledge, skills, and abilities (KSAs)** that are necessary to perform the job. It may also communicate the expected results of the position and explain how performance is evaluated. A job description, however, does not need to include every detail of how the work is performed. A **disclaimer section** typically discusses change in duties, performing duties not listed, and employment relationship. Table 3.3 lists the major components of a job description:

HELPFUL HINT

According to the ADA, a job description should list the essential functions of a job in order of importance.

TABLE 3.3. Components of a Job Description

SECTION	PURPOSE	EXAMPLES
General information	basic position and pay information, which may also be tracked in the HR Information System (HRIS)	job title position type (e.g., full time) FLSA status pay grade department direct supervisor direct reports job code
Position purpose	a summary of the position's essential functions and its role in relation to the department or organizational unit	description of the role relation to the department or organization estimated duration of position

56 Elissa Simon | SHRM CP EXAM PREP

SECTION	PURPOSE	EXAMPLES
Essential job duties	a list of duties and responsibilities (an essential function occupies a significant amount of the position's time and requires specialized skills to perform)	functions of the job, arranged by importance and percentage of time spent essential tasks related to the accomplishment of an essential function
Minimum requirements	the knowledge, skills, and abilities required to perform the essential functions of the job	education length of experience soft skills technical skills specific experience

Job Specifications

Job specifications list the KSAs needed to perform a role. Job specifications are often included within a job description, which typically focuses more on the particular tasks or duties of the role. The KSAs might include items such as educational requirements, personal abilities, experiences, physical requirements, and certifications.

Job Analysis

Understanding a job and developing a job description and job specifications is a process. This process is called **job analysis**. There are many ways that HR practitioners can perform a job analysis, such as interviewing the incumbent of a position, their manager, and their closest colleagues. HR professionals use a combination of interviews, job shadowing, questionnaires, and sample job descriptions to develop job descriptions for the organization. The job description must accurately reflect the essential duties and requirements of the job.

Different types of job analysis can be used to obtain different information about a role. A **task-based job analysis** focuses on specific steps a person takes to complete their duties. A **competency-based job analysis** looks at the specific skills or capabilities that an individual must possess to perform the job effectively. In addition to tasks and competencies, job analysis can also identify division of responsibilities that can be used in labor planning and determining department structures.

There are many methods of performing a job analysis, including observation, interviews, questionnaires, work sampling, or diaries. The type of job defines what method is most appropriate. An observation or work sampling might reveal enough information about a manual job because the duties and tasks can be watched easily. On the other hand, professional roles (e.g., accounting, legal) might require a questionnaire or diary to identify items that are not easily observed. The key is to identify not only daily but also weekly and yearly tasks that the role performs along with the KSAs needed to do the job.

 DID YOU KNOW?
FLSA status refers to the Fair Labor Standards Act. This differentiates exempt and nonexempt employees. Nonexempt employees must be paid overtime wages if they work over forty hours in a workweek.

When performing the job analysis, HR should consult several sources of information: the incumbent, the supervisor/manager, clients/customers, and other experts in the role. Job analysis steps include planning, introduction, and communication, conducting the job analysis, creating, and writing the job descriptions and job specifications, and maintaining records.

Physical requirements should be determined as part of the job analysis process and included in the job specifications. These physical requirements may be used as part of the recruitment process and to help identify any reasonable accommodations that might be made through the ADA.

EXAMPLES

5. Which of the following types of information is NOT typically included in a job description?

    A) a list of responsibilities

    B) FLSA status

    C) required skills

    D) company history

6. According to the ADA, a job description should list the essential functions of a job

    A) in order of percentage of time spent on a task.

    B) in order of importance.

    C) in no order at all.

    D) in alphabetical order.

Staff Planning and the Recruitment Process

Staff planning is a process by which an organization ensures it employs the right number of qualified people with the necessary skills to achieve organizational goals and objectives. Staffing plans require the cooperation of senior leadership, human resources, and management. The various components of a staff planning program include:

- job descriptions
- skills assessment of the current workforce (identifying gaps)
- turnover trends to predict how many people will leave an organization
- business trends examining both internal changes and the external factors

Once all relevant information has been collected, the human resources department (or staffing department in larger organizations) can forecast its staffing and recruitment needs. Typically, HR or staffing professionals work directly with business unit leads to interpret staffing metrics and forecast staffing data for the fiscal year.

There are a few important metrics in staffing and recruitment. The **selection ratio** is the number of available job positions compared to the number of applicants. On the other hand, the **yield ratio** is the ratio of applicants at one stage of hiring versus the number that moves on to the next stage. The **acceptance rate** is the percentage of candidates who accept a formal job offer.

Recruitment costs include items like cost of testing, background checks, relocation, and signing bonus. The total **cost of recruiting** is found by adding recruitment expenses for all the people hired. Ultimately, the **cost per hire** is found by dividing total recruiting costs by number of people hired.

During the planning process, HR and business unit leads will discuss the needs of the business unit, reevaluate jobs and processes, and identify a staffing model that supports the goals of the business unit. In some cases, a job may be redesigned, combined with another job, or divided into two or more jobs. The needs of the business as well as the available budget will determine how jobs are structured and how many employees a business unit will have during the year.

Applicant Tracking System

An **applicant tracking system (ATS)** is a program that automates the application and recruitment process. An ATS allows job seekers to find and apply for jobs by electronically submitting an application with a resume and cover letter attached. Data is collected from internal applications through the ATS interface. The ATS interface may also be linked to the company website or internet job boards to attract external applicants. Recruiters can post jobs, search through applications, track candidate progress, and communicate with applicants through the ATS.

The main function of an ATS is to provide a central location and database to support the company's recruiting activities. The ATS helps recruiters maintain resumes and applications and stay compliant with federal and state employment and document retention laws.

Recruitment Process

As jobs become available (through turnover or growth), organizations recruit candidates for these vacancies. The **labor market** is the pool of individuals an organization attracts as applicants or employees. The following is an overview of a typical recruitment process. Steps may vary depending on the organization.

1. Determine the recruitment process for the position: how many candidates will be identified, estimated timeline for filling the position, number of interviews, and composition of interviewing team.
2. Create or revise job descriptions to reflect the essential functions and requirements of the job.
3. Develop a job ad based on the job description that includes information about the company, salary range, preferred requirements, and/or benefits.
4. Identify candidate sources and begin the search. Post job ads to job boards, social media, classified sections of newspapers, at universities

and colleges, and other places where qualified candidates may be reached. Internal postings on a company intranet or bulletin board (for referrals) may be another method. Advertisements should include instructions for applying (e.g., an email address to submit resumes or an online application system).

5. Prescreen resumes and identify applicants who meet the qualifications of the job. The **applicant pool** is the total number of individuals who have been evaluated for selection. Develop a short list of candidates for further consideration.

6. Conduct an initial **phone screen** of shortlisted candidates and ask questions to understand their qualifications, gauge their interest, and evaluate their potential. Trim down the shortlist and invite the most qualified for an interview.

7. Interview candidates (with interviewing team) and ask probing questions to further evaluate their qualifications and fit for the position. In some cases, a second or even third interview is conducted for the finalist(s).

8. Conduct **preemployment tests**, references, and **background checks** of finalist(s) if necessary for the position or if required by the organization.

9. Make an offer of employment to the final candidate, including salary details, job role, responsibilities, benefits, start date, and other relevant information. In some cases, a verbal offer is made over the telephone and followed up with an **offer letter**, a written letter laying out the salary details, start date, and so on. It is always a best practice to send a written offer with the terms of employment and have it signed by the candidate.

10. In some cases, the candidate may negotiate salary, benefits, perks, office location, and other factors. When an agreement has been made, it is also a best practice to update the written offer letter and have the candidate sign it.

Once the candidate has accepted the terms and is preparing to begin work, the organization should take steps to ensure that the new employee is properly transitioned and integrated into the organization.

Onboarding

Once new employees are hired, they typically go through new hire training, or onboarding. **Onboarding** is the process of helping new hires integrate into their new work environment, learn their jobs, and transition into their roles. Onboarding is a critical component of the overall recruitment process for the employer and the employee.

Onboarding activities typically involve the following:

- a tour of the office or facility
- an overview of the organization—an explanation of the company's history; its products or services; and its mission, strategy, and vision

DID YOU KNOW?

Employers must screen candidates thoroughly. **Negligent hiring** is a legal theory that makes employers liable for a harmful act if the employer knew about the employee's potential to cause harm.

- completion of required HR and payroll forms, as well as benefits enrollment (if applicable)
- training on the rules, culture, and procedures of the organization
- on-the-job training and job shadowing
- mandated training on safety, sexual harassment, nondiscrimination, whistleblower, and other topics as required by law

In many cases onboarding typically lasts only a few days or weeks, but a robust onboarding process can span one to two years. This lengthier onboarding process will monitor the employee's progress, provide mechanisms for ongoing feedback, and help the employee understand how they fit into the organization as a whole. For many organizations, a lengthy onboarding process is integrated into their overall performance management program.

Depending on the structure, size, and resources of the organization, onboarding programs may be simple or complex. However, they should at least address the logistics, training, and safety of the new employee. New employees should have ample time training on the job and shadow others if possible, in order to gain a total understanding of the product or service. With a holistic understanding of the organization and its operations, as well as a foundational knowledge of their own jobs, new employees are better positioned for long-term success.

Managing the Workforce

Depending on the internal and external environment, an organization may face a surplus or shortage of talent.

In a **talent surplus**, the organization has more employees than it needs. During a talent surplus, employers must consider options like a hiring freeze, limiting the number of hires, limiting the number of hours worked, reducing compensation, and introducing a voluntary separation program. All are designed to control labor costs.

On the other hand, an organization faces a **talent shortage** when it cannot attract or retain enough workers to meet its needs. Short-term solutions to a talent shortage include outsourcing to a third party, using contingent workers, increasing employee hours through overtime, and initiating an employee referral program.

Separation occurs when an employee leaves the organization. Voluntary separation may include **resignation** or **retirement**. An employee who is **terminated** or fired is involuntarily separated from the organization.

HR can assist with separations in many ways. For instance, in case of a talent surplus, an organization may offer **voluntary layoffs**, in which staff are encouraged to voluntarily leave with **downsizing assistance** like payoffs, severance pay, or early retirement. **Outplacement services** provide support like interviewing workshops or career counseling for displaced workers.

HR conducts **exit interviews** with separating employees. Exit interviews are useful for gathering feedback about the organization and HR processes.

Turnover

Turnover refers to the number of employees leaving an organization and the reasons for their departure. There are three types of turnover: involuntary turnover, voluntary turnover, and controlled turnover.

When measuring turnover costs, HR should study the cost of separation, replacement, and training in addition to other hidden costs like employee morale, productivity impact, or customer satisfaction.

Outsourcing

Outsourcing simply means hiring outside contractors to do a job or certain tasks. **Recruitment agencies** find and screen candidates for organizations with small HR departments or that are short on time. However, they can be costly. An organization can achieve flexibility in staffing levels by using **independent contractors** during busy seasons or for specific projects. Additionally, using contractors allows the organization to work with individuals who are **subject-matter experts** in certain areas. A **professional employer organization (PEO)** supplies its own workforce to an employer, which can mean lower benefit costs for the employer, but higher operational costs and limitations on HR management.

EXAMPLE

7. Which of the following recruitment methods is likely to result in greater loyalty?
    A) campus recruiting
    B) internet job board
    C) employee referrals
    D) newspaper ad

Succession Planning

To remain viable and competitive, organizations must retain key talent to lead, manage, and execute their mission and vision. As employees resign, retire, or otherwise turn over, it is important for the organization to plan to keep its key positions filled with the most qualified people.

Succession planning is an organization's systematic approach to building a pool of future leaders to ensure leadership continuity. It develops potential successors in the leadership, identifies the best candidates for positions to meet future needs, and allocates resources to develop internal talent and create meaningful career paths.

Succession planning recognizes that some jobs are critical to the organization and therefore must be filled by the most qualified persons. Good succession planning is critical to mission success and sustains an effective process for recognizing, developing, and retaining top leadership talent.

The Succession Planning Process

1. **Align strategic planning with workforce planning.** Identify the long-term vision and direction of the organization, and analyze future needs to develop and offer products and services. Use data to understand the current composition of the workforce and to make projections for future workforce needs.

2. **Analyze gaps in future workforce needs.** Identify needs for competencies or skills, and determine talent needed for future demands. Develop a business plan based on long-term talent needs, not specific positions.

3. **Identify talent pools of current workforce and categorize talent based on career level, path, and potential.** Assess the competencies and skills of employees using formal appraisals and 360-degree feedback. Analyze external sources of future leadership as well.

4. **Develop strategies for succession**, including recruitment, relocation, and retention programs. Identify learning and development strategies, including job assignments, training programs, job shadowing, coaching and mentoring, and feedback mechanisms.

5. **Implement succession-planning strategies.** Maintain commitment and involvement of senior leadership. Communicate activities with employees regularly and actively.

6. **Monitor and evaluate succession-planning efforts.** Solicit and consider feedback from leadership as well as potential future leaders. Analyze employee satisfaction through surveys and informal feedback. Assess the responsiveness of the organization to change and to future needs.

Benefits of Succession Planning

Successful succession planning initiatives are based on the long-term needs of the business—they are an investment in the future. Senior leadership is invested in the process and helps to groom emerging leaders. Future leaders are also accountable for their own development. The pipeline of future leadership is based on anticipated needs. Careful analysis of the organization's workforce and needs guides the process, while the process itself creates meaningful career paths for employees, which can be a motivational tool. Finally, succession planning addresses workforce challenges like recruitment and retention.

EXAMPLE

8. Succession planning is important because it
   A) ensures that key roles in the company will not be vacant.
   B) provides feedback for all employees.
   C) requires managers to go through training.
   D) controls the company's operating budget.

Immigration in the Workplace

Under the **Immigration Reform and Control Act of 1986 (IRCA)**, it is illegal for an employer to hire any person who is not legally authorized to work in the United States. Employers must verify the employment eligibility of all new employees. For organizations of certain sizes, the IRCA also prohibits discrimination based on national origin (as does Title VII) as well as on citizenship status. The purpose of the law is to prevent employers from discriminating against job applicants based on their race, ethnicity, because they speak English with an accent, or other reasons related to national origin. The United States Citizenship and Immigration Services (USCIS), a component of the United States Department of Homeland Security, oversees and enforces immigration, including that which is employment related.

It is against the law to hire an employee if the employer is aware that the employee is not legally authorized to work in the United States, or if they are, in federal wording, an "unauthorized alien." Under the law, an "unauthorized alien" is a non-US citizen who either does not have status as a permanent resident in the US, or who is not authorized for employment in the US. One way employers avoid noncompliance with the law is to hire US citizens. A US citizen is not an "alien" (and therefore is not an "unauthorized alien").

Another way of avoiding noncompliance is to hire "authorized aliens," noncitizens who are authorized to work in the US. These include permanent residents (individuals who have a "green card") or those "aliens" who are authorized to work in certain conditions (through a **work visa**). Table 3.4 contains an overview of common work visas available to immigrant workers. For more details and the most current conditions, check uscis.gov.

TABLE 3.4. Types of Temporary Work Visas

VISA CATAGORY	DESCRIPTION
H-1B	Person in Specialty Occupation. Requires a college degree or its equivalent.
H-2A	Temporary Agricultural Worker. For temporary or seasonal agricultural work. Limited to immigrants from designated countries.
H-2B	Temporary Nonagricultural Worker. For temporary or seasonal nonagricultural work. Limited to immigrants from designated countries.
L	Intracompany Transferee. To work at a particular entity or location of the current employer in a managerial or executive role, or in a position requiring specialized knowledge. Requires one year of continuous employment by current employer within the past three years.
O	Individual with Extraordinary Ability or Achievement. For immigrant workers with extraordinary ability or achievement in business, science, arts, athletics, education, and other categories. Must demonstrate national or international acclaim and continue to work in their field of expertise. This category also includes people providing essential services in support of a worker in this category.

In general, a citizen of a foreign country who wishes to enter the United States must first obtain a visa (for a temporary stay or permanent residence). Temporary worker visas are specifically for people who want to enter the United States to work for a specific period of time (rather than permanently or indefinitely). Applications for all visas require the prospective employer to file a petition with USCIS. The petition must be approved in order for the visa to be issued. Hiring immigrants with approved visas is compliant with federal law, while hiring immigrants without authorization from USCIS is illegal and can result in substantial penalties.

USCIS Form I-9

Form I-9 is a government-issued form that documents the evidence of a new employee's authorization to work in the United States. It also certifies the employer's actions taken to verify the evidence. This form must be completed within the first three days of the employee's hire. However, if the employment is for less than three days, the form must be completed on the day of hire.

To validate an employee's ability to work, an employer's authorized representative must verify both the identity of the employee and the employee's status. Depending on the documentation, one or two documents may be required. Some documents (e.g., an unexpired US passport) prove both identity and authorization to work. Other documents (e.g., a driver's license) prove identity but do not prove authorization to work. Still other documents (e.g., Social Security card) prove authorization to work but do not prove identity. The instructions on the form indicate which documents are acceptable and which combination(s) of documents may be used to verify employment eligibility.

Documentation regarding I-9 verification must be kept for certain minimum periods of time as mandated by law—either for three years from the employee's date of hire or one year after the employee leaves, whichever occurs later.

E-Verify

E-Verify is an internet-based system managed by the federal government that allows employers to verify a person's employment eligibility electronically. E-Verify supplements Form I-9. Participation in E-Verify is voluntary for employers unless the company is a certain type of federal contractor or otherwise required to participate. Employers may only use E-Verify after making a hiring decision. It is illegal to use E-Verify for screening applicants or for other purposes not connected to verifying employment eligibility.

The E-Verify system confirms an individual's eligibility to work in the United States. If the system reports a "tentative non-confirmation" (TNC) for a new hire, it means that the system found possible problems in verifying the person's eligibility to work in the US. In that situation, the employee may contest the TNC, during which time the employer may not take adverse actions against the employee. If it is determined that the employee is in fact not eligible to work in the US, the employer may no longer continue to employ the individual.

EXAMPLES

9. Who is responsible for verifying that an employee is eligible to work in the United States?

    A) USCIS

    B) the Department of Labor

    C) the employer

    D) the employee

10. Which document confirms an employee's identity and verifies their eligibility to work in the US, for purposes of the I-9 form?

    A) unexpired US passport

    B) driver's license

    C) birth certificate

    D) foreign passport

Answer Key

1. **B)** The Equal Employment Opportunity Commission (EEOC) is an independent agency that enforces federal laws prohibiting employment discrimination.

2. **D)** The Equal Pay Act of 1963 makes it illegal to pay different wages to men and women if they perform equal work in the same workplace.

3. **D)** AAPs must be signed by a company officer and made available to employees and vendors.

4. **C)** Equal Employment Opportunity is a doctrine that prohibits discrimination in employment. Several laws exist to enforce EEO that apply to companies throughout the US. Affirmative action is not required of all businesses, but under Executive Order 11248, Section 503 of the Rehabilitation Act of 1973, and Section 4212 of the Vietnam Era Veterans' Readjustment Assistance Act, government contractors and subcontractors must provide affirmative action.

5. **D)** Company history is not typically included in a job description.

6. **B)** According to the ADA, a job description should list the essential functions of a job in order of importance.

7. **C)** Employee referrals are most likely to result in greater loyalty.

8. **A)** Succession planning recognizes that some jobs are critical to the organization and therefore must be filled by the most qualified persons.

9. **C)** The employer is responsible for verifying an employee's eligibility to work in the United States.

10. **A)** An unexpired US passport verifies both an employee's identity and their eligibility to work in the United States.

4 Compensation and Benefits

What Are Total Rewards?

Total rewards describe all the tools an employer uses to attract, motivate, and retain employees, including anything the employee perceives to be valuable as a result of working at the organization. There are five components of total rewards:

1. Compensation
2. Benefits
3. Work/Life Programs
4. Recognition Programs
5. Professional Development

Figure 4.1. The Five Components of Total Rewards

Depending on available resources, employers offer these various programs or components as part of a total compensation package to employees. A competitive and appropriate compensation package is key to retaining and motivating employees, who in turn will deliver performance and results for the organization.

67

To remain competitive, the organization should monitor its competitors' packages and overall industry. Salary and benefit surveys are reliable sources of data for an organization to determine its compensation and benefit programs.

Employee Life Cycle

The total rewards program encompasses the whole life cycle of an employee. The **employee life cycle** starts with attraction and recruitment, moves into onboarding, then development and retention through to separation or termination.

At every stage, the organization must consider each aspect of the total rewards program, including wages, benefits, recognition, and development, and consider how that aspect impacts the performance of the company and its employees. Additionally, as an employee moves through these life cycle stages, their needs may change as they are impacted by varying situations, abilities, and experiences. It is important that a total rewards program is dynamic enough to meet the needs of the five stages of the employee life cycle.

EXAMPLE

1. Health insurance benefits are a component of
    - A) total rewards.
    - B) organizational development.
    - C) work-life balance.
    - D) pay for performance.

Compensation

Employee **compensation**, sometimes referred to as **remuneration**, is the money employees receive in exchange for the work they perform or the time they work. Compensation can include a wage, salary, commissions, or bonuses. Cash compensation can be categorized as fixed pay, variable pay, or premium pay.

According to the Equal Pay Act of 1963, there are four basic compensable factors: effort, skill, responsibility, and working conditions. Other **compensable factors** include the skills, years of experience, licenses, value to the organization, and any other factors that determine the worth of the job. When determining employee compensation, all forms of remuneration should be considered: wages and salary, bonuses and variable pay, and other types of remuneration.

Pay Classifications

Employees can be paid either on a salaried or hourly basis. Salaried employees are paid a predetermined amount based on the expectations and outputs of the job. This is an annual amount paid in regular intervals throughout the year according to the pay schedule.

Hourly employees are paid for time worked. They are paid an amount based on the number of hours worked in a pay period. There are no minimum required hours that an employee must work, though benefit plans typically define part-time and full-time workers based on the number of hours worked.

According to the **Fair Labor Standards Act (FLSA)**, an employee can be considered exempt or nonexempt. **Exempt** employees are exempted from the FLSA, so that act does not apply to them. The FLSA has strict guidelines on what types of positions are exempted. **Nonexempt** positions have specific requirements, including paying overtime wages when an employee works more than forty hours in a workweek. (See chapter 3, "Workforce Planning and Management," and chapter 5, "Employee and Labor Relations," for more details on the FLSA.)

All hourly employees are nonexempt due to the nature of the classification, but salaried employees can be either exempt or nonexempt. A nonexempt employee is paid a fixed sum based on the annual salary. Nonexempt employees also receive overtime when they work more than forty hours in a workweek.

The amount of overtime pay an employee receives depends on how many hours they worked in a pay week, not a pay period. If a pay period goes over multiple weeks, the employer cannot use an average of hours to pay overtime. Rather, overtime must be calculated each week.

Additionally, some employers or union contracts pay overtime for over eight hours worked in a day. But the FLSA requires only that overtime be paid for over forty hours worked in a week.

Types of Compensation

Fixed pay, also called **base pay**, is nondiscretionary compensation. That means it does not fluctuate based on performance or results. It is linked to the organization's pay philosophy and structure and to market conditions; examples include salary pay and hourly wage.

Variable pay is compensation that changes directly with performance or results achieved. It is a payment based on a performance over a specified period of time and can be linked to either or both the employee's and employer's performance. Examples include commissions, bonuses, short-term incentives, stock options, performance-sharing incentives, and profit sharing. **Pay-for-performance** is when employees are rewarded for achieving goals. A **piece-rate system** rewards an individual on the number of units they produce.

Premium pay is compensation that is tied to nontraditional work schedules, shifts, and skills; premium pay is provided in addition to fixed pay. Some examples of premium pay are shift differential pay, weekend/holiday pay, on-call pay, and skill-based pay (see *Pay Increases*).

Deferred compensation means some of an employee's compensation is paid out long after the employee earns the money. Examples may be a pension plan or stock options.

The general term **direct compensation** typically refers to monetary payouts that have been discussed previously in regard to monies paid for work or time performed. On the other hand, **indirect compensation** refers to nonmonetary items paid for by the company for the employee. Indirect compensation is sometimes called "fringe benefits" and includes items like tuition reimbursements, gym memberships, mobile phones, or company cars.

Fringe benefits are taxable unless the law specifically excludes the benefit. Some excluded benefits are health and other similar insurances, educational assistance up to a specific dollar amount, qualified deferred retirement plans, and de minimis or low-cost gifts like coffee cups. Some common, taxable benefits include mileage reimbursement, moving expenses, and awards and prizes like gift cards.

Remuneration Data Analysis

When determining the compensation levels and structure, an organization needs to consider data from many different sources. Furthermore, the organization should compare this data with internal data to determine individual pay.

 DID YOU KNOW?
Many organizations will "mark up" the benefit so that the amount, once taxed, hits the targeted level of the benefit. This way, the company, not the employee, assumes the cost of taxation.

Comparable worth describes the idea that employees who perform roles or work with relatively the same value should be paid a similar wage. Historically, comparable worth has described **pay equity** between men and women ("equal pay for equal work"). Comparable worth can be established by using a formal pay structure and compensation philosophy.

When analyzing pay, it is important to consider both the internal and external market data. Analysis of current employee wages can determine internal alignment. **Internal alignment** compares the compensation level of one job with another within the same organization. On the other hand, **external competitiveness** assesses the pay level of an internal job in relation to the market value of that job more broadly. Finally, **internal consistency** uses job analysis, wage data, and job descriptions to analyze the relative value and pay of a role as it relates to other roles in the organization.

When determining pay and creating pay structures, it is important to consider both internal and external alignment. For instance, the market may indicate that a specific job is worth more than other jobs within the department. But your company may choose to pay this specific job below the market average in order to maintain the same level of pay within that department. By the same token, a job in high demand that is difficult to recruit may be paid more than others within a specific department based on market wages.

Any decision to create internal inequities must be based on data, including performance, so the decision can be supported.

Pay Structures

A company's **pay structure** refers to its method of administering pay. There are two common types of pay structures. The **internal equity method** pays based on the job's placement in the organizational hierarchy. In **market pricing**, each job's pay is tied to the prevailing market rate. If an employee is paid below the established pay range of a job, they are considered green-circled. If they are paid above the market rate, they are considered red-circled.

A **red-circled** employee typically has their pay held or receives smaller increases until the market or target pay level meets their salary. Employees can be overpaid for a number of reasons, including a demotion whereby wages were held at a previous level, or when an employee's skills do not keep up with the changing demands of a job.

A **green-circled** employee typically receives larger increases to help the individual catch up to the market or target. It is often difficult for an organization, due to cost, to move an employee to a targeted level in one year. Rather, when an employee is green-circled, a plan is put into place to move that employee up over the course of a few years.

A pay structure helps clarify the value the organization places on each role; it also shows why employees are compensated differently. Furthermore, a pay structure helps human resources personnel equitably administer the organization's overall pay philosophy. Additionally, the pay structure also helps HR professionals administer incentive compensation, especially for people with higher levels of responsibility and accountability.

The first step in establishing a pay structure is to create a compensation philosophy: a statement that articulates how the company wants to pay and reward employees. The compensation philosophy defines how the organization compensates employees relative to the market. A pay structure should align the compensation and benefit strategies with the mission, vision, and values of the company.

An organization may have a lag method in which it pays below average due to limited funds or a new business model. The company may want to *meet the market*, which means paying at average market rates. Or, the company might want to *exceed the market*, paying above average to attract and retain employees. Exceeding the market can be an important strategy for a high-tech company that needs to attract employees in high demand.

Factors to consider when creating a compensation philosophy include the size of the organization, the financial performance, turnover levels within the organization, and candidate availability. A compensation philosophy should also account for the total compensation of an employee (e.g., wages, variable compensation, and benefits).

After establishing a pay structure or a philosophy, the organization must perform job analysis to determine the content of a job and the knowledge, skills, and attributes (KSAs) to perform it. See chapter 3, "Workforce Planning and Management," for details on performing job analyses.

Organizations use the information obtained through the job analysis process to establish job descriptions. An accurate and up-to-date job description must be available during the compensation process so that the job and its required KSAs are properly represented when examining internal and external markets.

With the job analysis and the job description in place, the pay grades and pay bands can be established. These tools establish compensation of a role relative to other roles in the organization. The organization uses factors like level of responsibility, span of control, and required education to rank the roles within the company. It is important to look at the role itself rather than the individuals performing the job.

Pay grades are a system of establishing a range of compensation through a fixed framework. Minimum, middle, and maximum pay levels are determined. There may be anywhere from five to fifteen pay grades depending on the size and complexity of an organization. There is no set standard or number of grades. Instead, each organization must determine the number based on its own needs. Each job is then assessed a pay grade based on the established factors. This sets up a transparent pay progression for employees as they enter a new role and develop their skills and abilities.

Pay bands are similar to pay grades but include a broader segment of the roles. In general, there are fewer bands in a structure than grades. Pay bands can be used to determine pay for certain levels within an organization (e.g., entry level, mid-managers, and executives).

To establish pay structures and determine the appropriate pay levels for jobs, HR professionals typically conduct a structured **compensation analysis**. Steps of the compensation analysis are listed below:

TABLE 4.1. Compensation Analysis

1. DETERMINE PAYROLL BUDGET.

- Research merit increases and salary adjustments in the company and in the industry.
- Determine how many jobs need to be priced.
- Project upcoming payroll budgets to account for these adjustments.

2. BENCHMARK EACH JOB'S VALUE.

- Use salary surveys to match the compensation of the internal job to an external job with similar duties. Compare with other jobs in the same industry or geographical location.
- Determine the benchmarked value based on the organization's compensation philosophy. For example, if the organization decides to pay "at market," the fiftieth percentile should be reviewed.

3. CREATE SALARY RANGES AND PAY GRADES.

- Use the internal equity method to create a series of grades or bands, with wide ranges at the top of the structure and narrower ranges at the bottom. Each grade is tied to a different level of responsibility within the company.
- Pay grades should have a spread by which the employee can progress in his or her job. There should be a minimum and maximum amount for each pay grade. Typically, the midpoint of a given grade should be 15 percent higher than that of the lower grade.
- Slot jobs into pay grades based on their market value and/or relative value in the organization.

Pay Increases

An organization will rely on the pay structure to manage **pay increases**. Pay increases may occur on several different schedules: annually, by calendar year, at promotion, or randomly. At the time of a wage review, financial performance, market data, and internal grades or bands should be considered.

Organizations award increases based on performance or merit. A **merit adjustment** rewards high performance. Similarly, an organization might offer compensation to employees who exceed their duties in the form of **incentive pay**. **Skill-based pay** rewards employees for mastering new skills and is typically given to those who perform physical or production work.

Many organizations award annual increases based on inflation or a **cost-of-living adjustment (COLA)** increase. Each organization must consider culture and performance to determine the type of increases they would like to award. A **seniority adjustment** refers to pay adjustment based on an employee's length of service or seniority at the organization.

HELPFUL HINT

Do not confuse skill-based pay with pay-for-knowledge, which is a compensation system based on an employee's KSAs, not an increase or bonus.

Creating strong compensation models is dependent on good data. Internal data can be collected through a payroll or Human Resources Information System (HRIS). When looking at internal data, all factors such as overtime pay, variable compensation, and other forms of pay should be considered.

External data can be more challenging to collect depending on the demographics of a company's location(s) and the relevant types of jobs. When determining the validity of wage data, sources and statistics must be considered. It is good to ask questions such as, How was the data obtained? Is there enough data for a specific role to make it statistically valid? How does the stated role align with the job that is being evaluated?

The Bureau of Labor Statistics (BLS) publishes wage data on the national, state, and regional levels. This data is provided directly by employers. An organization can use other statistical and business surveys when conducting a wage survey, depending on the company's specialty. When looking at the data, it is important to look at the average, or mean, as well as the median: the middle of the highest and lowest points being reported. Having established a compensation philosophy, the organization can then use the data to establish pay structures and compensation levels.

The PESTLE model is useful to study external markets because it incorporates political, social, economic, and technological factors. (See chapter 1, "Business Strategy and Ethics," for more information on the PESTLE analysis.)

HELPFUL HINT

It is best to get wage data from a reputable source such as the Bureau of Labor Statistics (BLS), an association that runs surveys, or a paid service. Employee feedback can be useful, but employees themselves may provide biased information, intentionally or not.

Executive Compensation

To attract and retain the most qualified executive team, organizations sometimes offer a unique package of executive benefits and compensation for presidents, C-level executives, vice presidents, and senior directors. **Executive compensation** differs from packages offered to lower-level employees. Executive compensation packages often include:

- base salary
- bonuses or performance incentives
- signing bonus (e.g., cash bonus for joining the organization)
- stock options (employees receive the opportunity to buy stock in the company)

- income protection in the event of a company sale or liquidation
- predetermined severance package for termination without cause
- executive-only benefits (e.g., additional insurance coverage)
- company perquisites, or "perks" (e.g., club memberships, company car, or use of company plane)

As with any other compensation, executive compensation is negotiated between the potential executive and the employer. However, the structure or terms may be substantially different from the "regular" package offered to other employees. It may be specifically customized for the executive; that is, each executive has their own compensation structure.

Typically, executive salary and benefits are documented in an employment contract or agreement. This document outlines the terms of employment including the full spectrum of compensation, benefits, perks, performance incentives, and severance agreements. In contrast with an offer letter provided to a lower-level employee, **executive compensation agreements** are more detailed and contain a variety of benefits and perks not offered to other levels of employees.

Sales Compensation

Typically, an employee in a sales role has a full or partial compensation program that is tied to a sales commission program. That is, a salesperson is compensated based on the sales: They "receive a commission" or "get paid by commission." Each organization must consider its goals to determine the appropriate sales commission program. Commissions may be based on overall revenue, sales above budget, profit margin, or number of units sold. Additionally, a sales commission may be a percentage of an individual's overall compensation, or it may be the only monies or compensation paid to an employee.

Global Compensation

When offering compensation and benefits to international employees, companies need to be knowledgeable of the country or region's culture and regulations.

A centralized compensation structure can provide simplified financial planning, increased transparency in compensation practices, consistency in the enforcement of compensation practices, and reduced administrative expenses.

However, global companies must be able to manage variations in compensation structures due to economic factors, local expectations that dictate what compensation and benefits are expected of a population, and holiday schedules that impact the organization's operations and compensation of employees.

To ensure compliance with international customs, laws, and regulations, companies must address many issues surrounding the compensation of their global workforce.

Privacy and data regulations vary among countries. For instance, companies with employees in European Union countries must follow the **EU Data Protection Directive,** which restricts how personal information can be collected, stored, and shared. The EU also restricts the sharing of data with countries that do not have rigorous security standards.

Another important issue is **maintaining pay equity**. Base pay and traditional compensation structures vary from country to country. For example, in France base pay can include vacation pay and overtime payments. Regional differences must be factored in to the overall compensation program, and they must be accounted for when analyzing internal pay equity.

Accounting for **cost of living** is a major matter of global compensation. The value of a US dollar in a given country affects the pay levels of employees in that country. For example, a position paying sixty thousand US dollars in the United States may pay a local employee for the same work eleven thousand US dollars in another country due to the difference in cost of living.

Managing cultural differences is essential in effective global compensation. Appropriate communication with employees (especially with respect to their compensation and benefits) must be handled in accordance with the country's customs.

In some cases, the organization may decide to outsource its administrative payroll and HR functions for international employees in order to better manage the costs of operating abroad.

Another part of global compensation is the remuneration for expatriates living outside their home country. A global organization needs to develop a pay structure for its expatriate personnel. This may include base salary as well as housing, transportation, visits to the home country, cost-of-living allowances, assignment incentives, premiums, and allowances. Though standardization of expatriate compensation is desired, it is often difficult to achieve based on the actual assignment, length, assignment location, home country location, cost of living in each country, and more.

When considering expatriate base salary levels, there are a number of different approaches. In the home country approach, the home country's salary levels are used. In the host country approach, the host country's salary levels are used. Finally, in the headquarters-based approach, the salaries at the location of the headquarters are used. Another consideration is "where" the employee is paid. Will they be paid in the currency of their home country or the assignment country?

Due to the assignment, some expatriates are awarded a **hardship allowance** or hazard pay to incentivize living in difficult context. If a family is moved along with the employee there can be educational assistance for the children to attend specific schools or spousal support in finding a job in the new country.

Extreme differences in compensation and benefits between expatriate and local staff may negatively affect morale within the organization. It is important to consider not only the expatriate but also the local staff to ensure internal alignment within the organization.

Other factors to consider are insurance coverage while abroad, taxes, and employment laws and regulations. Finally, an employer must also be thinking ahead to repatriation and the impact of the assignment compensation when the employee returns to their home country.

EXAMPLES

2. In determining compensation structure, *meet the market* means that the company
   A) pays only salaries, not hourly.
   B) uses market analyses to determine compensation.
   C) pays at average market rates.
   D) leads its competitors in compensation.

3. Which of the following is NOT a category of exempt status under the FLSA?
   A) outside sales
   B) management
   C) hourly assistants
   D) executives

4. Which of the following is generally true about executive compensation?
   A) Executives receive a wider variety of compensation than other employees.
   B) Executives receive cheaper health insurance than other employees.
   C) Executives are guaranteed pay even if they do not work.
   D) Executives do not receive a base salary.

Payroll

Payroll departments manage employee compensation, including tax withholdings and deductions. Payroll administrators manage the following processes to ensure the proper and timely compensation of employees:

- calculating time cards
- calculating salaries, wages, reimbursements, commissions, bonuses, overtime, and retroactive pay
- tracking and paying company-paid holidays, vacation time, and sick time
- handling paycheck deductions for taxes, wage garnishment, insurance, and retirement savings
- coordinating with the accounting and finance department to report all payments and deductions accurately

While human resources and payroll are considered two distinct functions, they often work together and may be combined in smaller organizations. For example, when HR initiates the hiring of an employee, payroll introduces the employee's information to the payroll system, collects and processes the employee's tax withholdings and deductions, and adds the employee onto the roster for paycheck processing.

Smaller organizations may outsource their payroll and/or human resources duties to **third-party administrators (TPA)**. A TPA can help the organization administer payroll, benefits, and HR records for less cost than hiring full-time staff. Other organizations, especially growing ones, may employ an internal staff member (such as an office manager) to act as a liaison between employees and TPAs to ensure that administration is handled accurately and quickly. Even larger companies may outsource all or part of their payroll or HR functions if it is in the best interest of the organization's budget, operations, and long-term goals.

Organizations often include both human resources and payroll management in the strategic planning process to ensure that those processes are closely aligned with the strategic goals of the organization. For example, human resources leadership can develop the appropriate strategies to attract, hire, and retain the best employees for the company. Meanwhile, payroll can develop strategies to streamline processes, ensure high accuracy in recordkeeping, and provide excellent service to employees. Both functions collaborate to conduct or assist in internal audits to ensure the accuracy of employee records and employment practices such as paying employees.

A **paycheck** or **pay stub** typically summarizes the amount of pay, deductions, taxes, and year-to-date compensation information. However, many employees find it difficult to fully understand their overall compensation when benefits and other fringes are included.

One communication device that helps show an employee the value of their total compensation package is a compensation statement. A **compensation statement** includes information about pay as well as information about direct and indirect compensation and benefits, including both the employer's and the employee's contributions. These figures are communicated as an annualized number for clarity.

When administering, running, or managing payroll, it is important to understand basic accounting principles. These ensure that the payroll, when integrated into the financial statements, is balanced and accurate. Payroll will impact several financial reports. The **balance sheet** is a financial summary of a company's assets and liabilities. The **profit and loss statement (P&L)** summarizes the organization's revenue, costs, and expenses. The P&L shows overall profitability and performance.

HELPFUL HINT

The P&L is sometimes known as the *income statement*.

The payroll function might also work directly with accounting in regard to **accounts payable**, or the money that is owed *by* the company, and the **accounts receivable**, the money owed *to* the organization. This might be especially true when working with an outsourced payroll organization and managing the flow of monies to the employees from the employer's bank accounts.

The payroll function will need to understand the **basic accounting principles** on which the organization's accounting standards and processes are built. This may include the *accrual principle*, in which the financial statements reflect the costs when they occur rather than when they are paid. In this type of system, even if a pay run falls into the next month, the cost of that payroll will be recorded in the month the hours were worked. Other principles would record the cost of the payroll only when it is actually paid. Knowing how the organization operates is key to effectively manage and record payroll.

EXAMPLE

5. An employee comes to HR upset because his pay stub shows large deductions for taxes, social security, Medicare, and health insurance. He feels that he is not getting his full compensation. What is the BEST way for HR to clarify the employee's annual compensation, including deductions and employer and employee contributions?

   A) several months' worth of pay stubs

   B) the employee's W2

   C) a compensation statement

   D) instruct the employee to speak with his supervisor

DID YOU KNOW?

Severance plans must comply with the Employee Retirement Income Security Act (ERISA). ERISA regulates employers who offer pension or welfare benefit plans to their employees. See later in this chapter, and see chapter 5, "Employee and Labor Relations," for details on ERISA.

Severance Pay

Severance pay is payment awarded to employees upon their termination. Its purpose is to help the terminated individual bridge the gap between jobs while they look for their next position. Though there is no one formula to compute the severance pay amount, it is usually based on length of service. Typically, the amount of severance is equal to one or two weeks of pay for every year of service.

Severance pay can be paid in one lump sum or it can be paid over several weeks. Additionally, a severance package might include an extension of benefits or the company paying the COBRA premium for the terminated employee.

Strategically, severance pay should be tied to a severance agreement, which is a contract made between the terminated employee and the organization that releases claims toward the employer for a specific amount of money or benefits.

Severance pay can affect a worker's unemployment because it is considered income by many state plans. Typically, unemployment is impacted the week or weeks that the severance is allocated.

Executive severance agreements or packages are aimed at the top executives of an organization. These protect an executive who is an at-will employee who is terminated without good cause. These agreements are typically agreed upon at time of hire and provide monetary protection for an executive who is asked to leave the organization. Reasons for termination without good cause, that is, for performance, may include downsizing, plant closings, mergers, acquisitions, or avoidance of a lawsuit.

Executive severance agreements are more generous than a typical severance pay and can include pay from six months to a year or more. They also may include bonuses and benefits.

Benefits

Employee benefits are important to the livelihood of employees and their families. Benefits not only support employees with their health, financial, and personal needs; they also make a total compensation package competitive and rich. The benefits an employer offers may be a deciding factor to convince a talented individual to work at the organization.

There are two categories of **employee benefits**: those that must be provided by law (also called **mandated benefits**) and those that the employer chooses to offer as a way to compensate employees (or to comply with a collective bargaining agreement in a unionized environment). Examples of mandated benefits include workers' compensation and unemployment insurance; optional benefits include health insurance coverage (in some cases) and retirement plans.

Mandated Benefits

The following table provides an overview of benefits that are **mandated** by federal law. (Certain health-related benefits are covered in more depth later in this chapter in the section "Health and Welfare Benefits.") Note that some states may require additional benefits for workers in those states.

TABLE 4.2. Mandated Benefits

MANDATED BENEFIT	PURPOSE
Social Security Taxes	Social security funds retirement income. Employers must pay social security taxes at the same rate paid by their employees.
Unemployment Insurance (UI)	Workers who become unemployed through no fault of their own and meet other requirements under state law receive UI. States administer their own UI programs under federal guidelines.
Workers' Compensation Insurance	Employees who become injured or ill due to their job receive workers' compensation benefits to cover payment for lost wages and medical bills. Employers must carry workers' compensation insurance coverage through an insurance carrier, on a self-insured basis, or through the state's program.
Disability Insurance	Certain states require businesses to provide insurance for wage loss due to employees' non-work-related sickness or injury. These benefits provide partial income replacement during the period of disability.
Family and Medical Leave	The Family and Medical Leave Act (FMLA) provides up to twelve weeks of unpaid leave to eligible employees for: 1. birth and care of the employee's child, or placement for adoption or foster care of a child 2. care of an immediate family member (spouse, child, parent) who has a serious health condition 3. care of the employee's own serious health condition The employee maintains group health benefits during the leave.
Military Family Leave	The FMLA was amended in 2008 to provide protections specifically for military families. Eligible employees receive up to twenty-six weeks of leave to care for injured family members and up to twelve weeks to tend to matters related to deployment. These leaves are also unpaid, but the employee maintains group health benefits.
Patient Protection and Affordable Care Act (PPACA)	PPACA requires employers with more than fifty employees to provide affordable health insurance that provides minimum value to their full-time employees (and their dependents).

Health and Welfare Benefits

Health and welfare benefits are the most common discretionary benefits offered by employers. Health and welfare benefits are typically offered in the form of a group health plan established or maintained by the employer (or union). They provide medical care for participants (and often their dependents) directly or through insurance, reimbursement, or otherwise.

The following are health and welfare benefits that employers may offer to their employees as part of their total compensation package:

- medical plan
- dental plan
- vision plan
- prescription drug plan
- flexible spending account (FSA)
- health reimbursement account (HRA)
- health savings account (HSA)
- life insurance
- accidental death and dismemberment insurance
- short- and long-term disability insurance

HELPFUL HINT

Remember, employers with more than fifty employees are subject to the PPACA; health care becomes a mandated benefit.

Most welfare plans can be provided by an employer to its employees on a pretax basis (meaning the cost of the plan is not taxable to the employee). As an exception, some welfare plans will result in additional gross income to a highly compensated employee or a key employee unless the plan meets the nondiscrimination requirements determined by the Internal Revenue Code. A few benefits and plans are listed in more detail below.

A **cafeteria plan** allows an employee to reduce their compensation in order to pay their share of employer-provided benefits coverage on a pretax basis. In a cafeteria plan, employees can choose from two or more cash or qualified benefit plans (hence the name *cafeteria*). Pretax benefits like health insurance, group-term life insurance, flexible spending accounts, and certain voluntary supplemental benefits (e.g., dental or vision coverage) could all be available through the plan. A cafeteria plan must not discriminate in favor of either highly compensated employees or key employees.

HELPFUL HINT

A cafeteria plan is sometimes called a Code Section 125 plan or a flexible benefits plan.

In a **flexible spending account (FSA)**, an employee sets aside a portion of earnings to pay for certain expenses as established in the cafeteria plan. Usually, employees use an FSA for medical expenses, but FSAs can also apply to dependent care or other expenses. FSA contributions are made on a pretax basis. The FSA is a "use it or lose it" program whereby the unused dollars are not available to the employee after the plan year. Rather, these dollars either go back to the employer to offset the administration costs or are distributed to all the participants of the plan depending on the plan design.

A **health reimbursement account (HRA)** is an employer-funded account that can be used to cover qualified medical expenses of the employee and their dependents. This account may be used to pay for the participant's out-of-pocket, qualified medical expenses until insurance covers the expense or the funds are depleted.

A **health savings account (HSA)** is a pretax medical savings account available to participants in a high-deductible health plan (HDHP). The funds contributed to an account are not subject to federal income tax upon deposit. Funds are used to pay for the participant's out-of-pocket, qualified medical expenses (and those of their dependents). This account can roll over year after year, allowing the employee to build a balance for future medical needs.

Employers (as plan administrators and/or fiduciaries) and their health plans must comply with several health- and welfare-related federal laws.

- The **Employee Retirement Income Security Act (ERISA)** covers most private-sector health plans. ERISA provides protections for participants and beneficiaries covered under employee benefit plans. Plan administrators and fiduciaries are required to meet certain standards of conduct that are outlined in the law.

- The **Consolidated Omnibus Budget Reconciliation Act (COBRA)** grants employees the right to keep the group health insurance (and pay the premium) that they would otherwise lose after they quit or lose their jobs, or reduce their work hours. Most people can retain their insurance coverage for up to eighteen months (and longer, in some situations).

- The **Health Insurance Portability and Accountability Act of 1996 (HIPAA)** provides opportunities for people to retain (or obtain) health insurance during qualifying events. It also protects the confidentiality and security of health care information and provides mechanisms to control administrative costs.

- As discussed in Table 4.2, the **Patient Protection and Affordable Care Act (PPACA)** requires certain employers to offer affordable health insurance that provides minimum value to their full-time employees and their dependents. Employers must also communicate about health care marketplaces to employees and offer a standardized summary of coverage to employees (among other requirements). Insurers must cover preexisting conditions and cover all applicants.

- The **Pregnancy Discrimination Act (PDA)** requires certain health plans to provide the same level of coverage for pregnancy as for other conditions. (See chapter 3, "Workforce Planning and Management," for more details on the PDA.)

- The **Mental Health Parity Act** requires that when a health plan covers mental health services, the annual or lifetime dollar limits, copays, and treatment limitations must be the same as or higher than the limits for other medical benefits.[1]

- The **Americans with Disabilities Act (ADA)**, among other protections, requires that disabled and nondisabled individuals

---

1   "Mental Health Parity," US Department of Labor, accessed August 19, 2015, **http://www.dol.gov/ebsa/mentalhealthparity/**.

be provided the same benefits, premiums, deductibles, and limits under a given health plan. (See chapter 3, "Workforce Planning and Management," for more details on the ADA.)

- As discussed in Table 4.2, the **Family and Medical Leave Act (FMLA)**, among other protections, requires that an employer maintain health coverage for a qualified employee for the duration of FMLA leave.

- The **Uniformed Services Employment and Reemployment Rights Act (USERRA)**, among other protections, allows employees to continue group health coverage while absent from work due to military service. (See chapter 5, "Employee and Labor Relations," for more information on USERRA.)

Time-Off Benefits

Employers may offer personnel several types of time-off benefits. These benefits include both paid-time-off and unpaid-time-off benefits. **Paid time off** is when the employee receives continuation of pay while away from work due to agreed-upon reasons.

Paid time off can mean paid vacation time, sick days, personal time, or holidays. Some organizations offer nontraditional paid time off such as paying for volunteer days and exercise or wellness time. **Sabbaticals** are paid extended leaves for job development or rejuvenation. More companies are offering **paternity leave** or simply nongendered parental leave.

An employer may also offer a leave program. This may be an unpaid or paid leave from work. A **leave** is time off from work due to a specific reason. The most common leaves include those for sickness, birth of a child, bereavement or funeral, and jury duty.

Leaves may coincide with other paid benefits like disability or workers' compensation programs. Or, the employer may choose to pay the employee a certain amount during the leave. Other times, the leave is taken unpaid with an agreement about returning to work within a specific period of time.

Employers with more than fifty employees are subject to the FMLA. The FMLA covers leaves for the birth or adoption of a child, a serious health condition of the employee or immediate family, or military family leave for the care of a wounded service member or exigency. The FMLA offers job protection to employees for up to twelve weeks (or longer in the case of military family leave). Under the FMLA, employees on leave are guaranteed their job back, though they are not guaranteed compensation for the time on leave. That is, these leaves may be unpaid. To qualify for FMLA leave, the employee must have been employed at the company for at least twelve months and have worked a minimum of 1,250 hours in those past twelve months.

Many employers have moved away from the traditional siloed time-off programs such as vacation, personal time, and sick days to a more consolidated **paid-time-off (PTO)** benefit. In a PTO program, the employees are awarded a higher number of hours to use when away from work with the expectation that this time be used for most absences. The employees' vacation, sick days, jury duty, bereavement, and personal days are typically all rolled into PTO. Rather than pulling from multiple accruals or programs, the time is managed by just one plan.

Income Replacement Programs

There are a number of income replacement programs, both legally mandatory and voluntary, that organizations offer employees to ensure financial support if the employee is unable to work.

Mandatory income replacement benefits include **workers' compensation**, which is paid when a worker is injured or becomes ill out of the course of employment, and **unemployment insurance (UI)**. In most states, workers' compensation insurance is purchased by the employer. Some states have state-run plans that the employer contributes to rather than buying an insurance policy.

Employers pay both federal and state unemployment taxes. Individuals can collect unemployment when they are ready and willing to work but are unable to due to a termination of employment for reasons beyond their control (e.g., layoffs, job elimination). Generally, employed workers will not qualify for unemployment benefits if they left their jobs voluntarily, if they are unable to work, or if they were fired for cause.

Voluntary income replacement programs include leaves-of-absence benefits.

Retirement Benefits

In addition to health and welfare plans, many organizations also offer retirement plans to their employees. A **retirement plan** is a savings plan that supports employees once they retire. Retirement plan income replaces employment income. These plans may be set up by employers, unions, or other institutions. Retirement plans fall under three categories: defined benefit plans, defined contribution plans, and profit-sharing plans.

- **Defined benefit plans** are company-provided pension plans in which an employee's pension payments are calculated (defined) according to the employee's length of service with the company and their earnings prior to retirement.
- **Defined contribution plans** are retirement savings plans in which the employer or employee (or both) contributes on a regular basis (typically pretax, assuming certain conditions are met). There is no guaranteed benefit. Employees have limited access to their accounts until retirement, though there may be a loan provision in the plan or hardship withdrawals. Typically, any withdrawal before the age of fifty-nine and a half is penalized.

Examples of defined contribution plans include individual retirement accounts: IRA, 401(k), and 403(b) programs. These are governed by the IRS and are subject to specific tax regulations. An employee's ability to transfer money from one retirement account to another if they change jobs ("rollover") depends on the organization's vesting schedule.

- **Profit-sharing plans** are typically offered in conjunction with a defined contribution plan. They allow the company to allocate profit to the employees' retirement accounts using a predetermined formula and vesting schedule.

Retirement plans may have a vesting schedule. When an employee vests, it means they have rights or ownership to the monies within a plan. With 100 percent vested, they have 100 percent ownership to that money.

There are two types of vesting schedules: cliff and graded. A **graded schedule** means an employee earns a specific percentage ownership to the company contributions until 100 percent vesting is met. This can take up to six years within a defined contribution plan. A **cliff vesting schedule** is one in which the employee is 100 percent vested upon reaching a specific milestone. This may be immediately upon hire or after reaching a designated anniversary year.

Fiduciary Responsibility

Under the Employee Retirement Income Security Act (ERISA), the owner, CEO, CFO, or even the human resources representative may have **fiduciary responsibility**. That is, they are held accountable for decisions that are made around the company's retirement plans.

A **fiduciary** can be anyone who has authority or control over the administration of an ERISA employee benefit plan such as a 401(k) program. The "prudent man rule," or "prudent person rule," insists that the fiduciary invests another person's assets as they would their own, with caution and care. An individual who does not meet the "prudent man standard of care" may face civil penalties or even lawsuits. That is, decisions around the plan were not made with the employees' best interests in mind.

EXAMPLES

6. Which of the following is typically considered a taxable benefit?
    A) vacation pay
    B) health insurance
    C) flexible spending account
    D) 401(k) matching contribution

7. COBRA allows a terminated employee to continue coverage under the employer's health insurance policy for how long?
    A) twelve months
    B) eighteen months
    C) thirty-six months
    D) indefinitely

8. The prudent person rule is associated with which law?
    A) FLSA
    B) ERISA
    C) FMLA
    D) OSHA

Work-Life Balance Programs

As business demands continue to increase in the global economy, high-performing employees risk burnout. To manage and limit burnout, organizations offer **work-life balance programs** to help employees integrate work and family life through nontraditional work arrangements, counseling and support, and concierge services. **Employee assistance programs (EAPs)** provide independent, confidential, and free counseling and support services in mental health; family life; and financial, legal, and other issues.

Companies with greater resources may also offer dry cleaning, child care, on-site fitness centers, and other perks to help employees stay balanced. Additionally, flexible work schedules, job sharing, telecommuting, and compressed workweeks can make it easier for employees to balance family needs while performing well at a minimal cost to the organization.

EXAMPLE

9. What is the purpose of an employee assistance program (EAP)?
    A) to provide free, confidential counseling on work-life and personal matters
    B) to assist employees with finding a job when they are laid off
    C) to help employers find the best candidates for a position
    D) to provide legal counsel to employees who want to sue the company

Recognition Programs

Recognition programs can have a significant impact on business performance and employee morale. Some organizations have formal recognition programs with monetary rewards; others offer informal or low-cost recognition programs. Regardless of budget, successful recognition programs share the following characteristics:

1. They reward results or behaviors such as meeting sales targets, saving the company significant money, completing an important project, or otherwise affecting the business in a notably positive way.
2. They give feedback that is immediate and frequent, providing positive reinforcement for positive behaviors; furthermore, they can be used as a motivational tool.
3. They offer opportunities for peer-to-peer recognition, creating a positive team dynamic, camaraderie, and strong working relationships.
4. Recognition is public and is embedded into the company's values. When employees are recognized publicly by leadership, they feel appreciated and essential to the company's success.

A culture of recognition is an important tool to retain good employees and motivate new ones. Moreover, when employees celebrate their successes together, synergy in the workplace improves.

Finally, recognition programs help meet basic psychological needs. Psychologist Abraham Maslow theorized that human beings have a series of needs (**Maslow's hierarchy of needs**). These range from the most basic (physical needs) to the most complex (self-actualization). Maslow's hierarchy of needs is depicted below showing the levels of needs each human being must satisfy to reach psychological fulfillment.

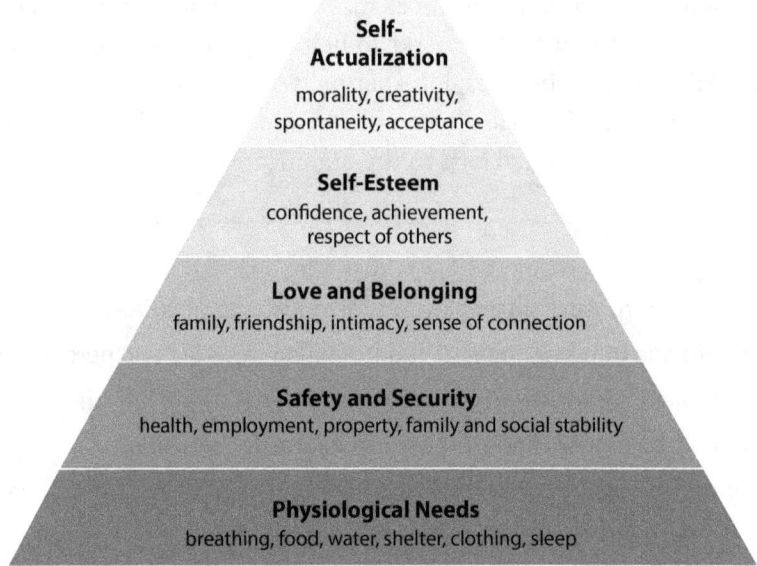

Figure 4.3. Maslow's Hierarchy of Needs

According to Maslow's theory, two of the most important psychological needs of humans are the need for appreciation and the need to belong. Organizations can meet these psychological needs through recognition programs. Having psychological needs met is an important element of an employee's decision to remain at an organization.

Professional Development Programs

Professional development refers to the acquisition of skills and knowledge, both for personal development and for career advancement. It can take the form of formalized training programs, external training opportunities, and financial assistance with work-related degree programs. Below are some examples of common **professional development programs** that companies offer to employees:

- training seminars and workshops (internal)
- external seminars and workshops
- tuition assistance for advanced (work-related) degrees
- reimbursement for certification exams and recertification fees
- mentoring
- career coaching

Professional development programs are key to a competitive total rewards package and are mutually beneficial to the employee and the employer. Employees acquire new skills and knowledge improving their work, advancing them in the organization, and increasing their competitiveness in the marketplace. (In some cases, professional development activities are required to maintain mandatory professional certifications.) Employers benefit with a smarter, more efficient workforce that can attain higher goals; employers may also benefit through reduced costs, thanks to improved innovation and operational efficiency.

Other Benefits

In addition to major health, welfare, and retirement benefits, companies may also offer voluntary benefits to employees, such as critical illness coverage, long-term care coverage, wellness programs, automotive insurance, home insurance, and other coverage at a group discount. These programs might be purchased by the individual employee through a payroll deduction program or bought by the organization itself.

Other benefits may include pet benefits, student debt forgiveness programs, or new parent programs. Offering a complete package of benefits to suit the various needs of employees helps attract well-qualified talent to the organization and can be used as a retention tool as well.

EXAMPLE

10. What is the main reason employers offer a comprehensive benefits package?

- **A)** to reduce operating costs
- **B)** to do what other companies are doing
- **C)** to help attract and retain employees
- **D)** to save money on taxes

Answer Key

1. **A)** The term "total rewards" refers to compensation, benefits, work-life programs, recognition programs, and professional development.

2. **C)** "Meet the market" means the company pays at average market rates.

3. **C)** Hourly workers are nonexempt under the FLSA.

4. **A)** Executives generally receive not only higher compensation than other employees but also more variety in compensation (stock options, signing bonus, income protection, executive-only bonus, predetermined severance package, and perks).

5. **C)** In this situation, the best solution would be to offer the upset employee a compensation statement. An overview of his annual compensation, including employer and employee contributions, and a clear explanation of mandated benefits and required deductions like taxes, could help him better understand his net pay and the actual cost of certain benefits like health insurance. He could also see what his employer contributes. He might not have a full understanding of the costs of certain taxes. A compensation statement could clear up his concerns.

6. **A)** Compensation is taxable even if it is for paid time off.

7. **B)** COBRA coverage allows a terminated employee to continue coverage under the employer's health insurance policy for up to eighteen months in most cases.

8. **B)** In HR, the prudent person rule is mainly associated with ERISA. A fiduciary should invest according to the prudent person rule, managing employees' retirement assets with care.

9. **A)** EAPs provide employees with counseling on work-life and personal matters. Along with work-life balance programs, they help reduce burnout.

10. **C)** A comprehensive benefits package attracts and retains the most talented employees.

5 Employee and Labor Relations

Employee and labor relations is concerned with maintaining positive employer-employee relationships to ensure high productivity and morale. **Employee relations** refers to the relationship between management and employees. **Labor relations** is the term used to discuss a unionized environment.

HR professionals perform employee relations when they work with an organization to create and maintain a positive culture. This could include advising managers on handling poor performance or employee misconduct. However, employee relations should focus on the proactive activities that ensure strong relationships between the employees and the organization. This might include creating a strategic plan to implement cultural goals, ensuring good communication throughout the organization, designing workplace activities to build relationships, or conducting surveys to understand current employee issues or morale.

But the HR professional should also understand federal labor law, the history of organized labor in the United States, and protections for workers. HR also plays a role in resolving disputes and grievances, and disciplining and terminating employees. Ensuring these activities are done in a fair, legal, and consistent manner can support a positive culture.

Labor Relations

The term **labor relations** refers to the interaction between employers and bargaining unit employees in a unionized environment (however, in some cases it applies to nonunion workers as well). Labor relations, like employee relations, also examine how employees are affected by economic factors like globalization and recession, and strive to minimize their negative impact on the workforce.

When labor relations are strong at an organization, management works effectively with employee representatives (typically labor unions) to solve problems among the employees and the organization. For example, if the cost of materials rises substantially and threatens mass layoffs, the labor relations process could find ways to cut costs elsewhere; adapt to the changes; and innovate new, sustainable products or business strategies; thereby protecting jobs.

In the United States, labor is closely regulated by federal and state law. Under the National Labor Relations Act (NLRA), **unfair labor practices** are defined as acts that violate the NLRA. These include discrimination, coercion, and intimidation prohibited to both labor and management. For example, management cannot form company unions or use coercive tactics to discourage union organization. Unions negotiate many aspects of the workplace through contracts with management. For instance, a worker's length of service with an employer is called **seniority**. In union contracts, seniority often determines layoffs from work and recalls back to work.

On a global level, the International Labour Organization (ILO), the only tripartite UN agency, brings together governments, employers, and workers from 187 member states. The purpose of this organization is to set standards, develop policies, and devise programs to promote fair and equitable work for men and women around the world. The mission statement of the ILO is "to promote rights at work, encourage decent employment opportunities, enhance social protection and strengthen dialogue on work-related issues" (www.ilo.org).

Organized Labor in the Workplace

An organized workplace can take a number of different formats, types, and structures. Organized labor, or labor unions, is a single entity that represents member employees collectively. These unions can be organized vertically or horizontally.

Horizontal unions, also known as **trade unions**, are composed of workers across the same industry rather than within a single business or organization. Examples of horizontal unions include the International Brotherhood of Electrical Workers (IBEW) or the United Brotherhood of Carpenters.

Vertical unions, also known as **industrial unions**, allow workers in various positions practicing different crafts to join. Membership is determined by industry or geographic location. Examples of these types of unions are the International Brotherhood of Teamsters or the United Automobile, Aerospace and Agricultural Implement Workers of America (UAW).

On a global level, worker representation can take on different forms. Many countries legislate work councils, which may or may not be within a unionized setting, that create local representation within an organization. You might also see trade union federations where local trade unions are affiliated with a national organization.

Labor unions use tools to negotiate with management. Their greatest strength is in their bargaining power. A **bargaining unit** is a group of employees who bargain collectively with their employer (i.e., through a union). **Collective bargaining** is a negotiation process between the union and the employer about wages and other conditions of employment. Generally, if a company wants to change the terms of a collective bargaining agreement while it is in effect, it must give sixty days' notice. If the union and management cannot resolve a dispute, it may go to arbitration. **Arbitration** is the referral of disputes to an impartial third party (an arbitrator rather than court). The arbitrator's decision is typically final and binding.

If bargaining fails, unions take other actions. **Picketing** is the public protest of an employer by workers, discouraging non-striking workers and customers to enter the business. Picketing typically takes place during a **strike**, when the bargaining unit refuses to work until a collective bargaining agreement is reached. Unionized workers may also engage in **boycotts**, when groups refuse to buy certain goods or services to put pressure on a supplier. On the other hand, management may respond to organizing workers in the form of a **lockout**: closing a facility to coerce workers to meet a demand.

Some workplaces are unionized, some are not, and some are partially unionized. These statuses are determined by a union security clause. A **union security clause** is a clause in the collective bargaining agreement that provides for a union shop, maintenance of membership, or an agency shop. Union contracts may include a union security clause stating that as a condition of employment, workers must be members in good standing of the union. This may include payment of union dues and fees.

In an **open-shop** workplace, people are employed without respect to union membership. In a **union shop**, the employer is allowed to hire individuals who are not currently members of the union with the provision that they are required to join the union after a specified amount of time. In an **agency shop**, an employee is not required to join the union, but they are still obligated to pay dues or fees to the union. Finally, a **closed shop** refers to the practice of hiring only individuals who are current union members. Closed-shop workplaces were made illegal under the federal law (the Taft-Hartley Act, page 97).

Some states have **right-to-work laws**. These laws prohibit or limit union agreements that require employees' membership, or payment of union dues or fees, as a condition of employment. Despite their name, these laws do not provide a general guarantee of employment.

Collective bargaining agreements typically include a provision for union stewards to represent the members at a local level. A **union steward** is usually a volunteer position that may be elected by the members. There may be one or more stewards depending on the contract and size of the organization. Stewards may receive some preferential treatment in the event of a layoff. They may be paid by the employer for reasonable union activities.

 DID YOU KNOW?

Collective bargaining among federal workers was legalized by **Executive Order 10988**, which allows federal employees to collectively bargain with management. It was signed by President John F. Kennedy.

EXAMPLES

1. What is the greatest strength of a labor union?
    A) collective bargaining
    B) union dues
    C) right-to-work laws
    D) strikes and lockouts

2. How much notice must a company give the bargaining unit if it wants to change the terms of a collective bargaining agreement while it is in effect?
   A) 30 days
   B) 60 days
   C) 90 days
   D) 120 days

3. Which union security clause requires workers to join a union?
   A) closed shop
   B) union shop
   C) open shop
   D) agency shop

4. State right-to-work laws limit or prohibit which of the following?
   A) formation of unions
   B) termination of employment
   C) unfair labor practices
   D) union shops

Labor Relations in Federal Law

Labor relations are regulated by the US government, which provides guidance on the treatment of employees. The **National Labor Relations Act (NLRA) of 1935**, also called the **Wagner Act** or **Wagner-Connery Labor Relations Act**, is enforced by the **National Labor Relations Board (NLRB)**. This act granted most private-sector workers several labor rights, including the right to strike, to bargain as a union, and to protest the conditions of their employment. It does not apply to management, government employees, independent contractors, and certain other employees.

Employees covered by the NLRA are granted certain rights to join together to improve their wages and working conditions, with or without a union. This means that although a union may not be present in an organization, employees at that organization still have the right to discuss the conditions of their employment and to take action as a group.

Under the NLRA, employees have the right to form a union if one does not already exist. If they no longer support an existing union, they have the right to stop recognizing, or *decertify*, it. In exchange for membership dues, the union represents employees on matters related to their pay, benefits, and workplace conditions. The union will assist employees when they file complaints or grievances, or when an employer is not abiding by a collective bargaining agreement. It is illegal for employers to retaliate against employees who form a union or who engage in a protected activity covered under the NLRA.

The NLRA also protects employees who are not represented by a union but are engaged in concerted activity. **Concerted activity** occurs when two or more employees take action to protect themselves in the workplace or improve their work situation. For example, concerted activity may involve a group of employees asking a manager to raise their wages. It may also apply to two or

HELPFUL HINT

TIPS stands for "threats, interrogation, promises, and surveillance." The NLRB prohibits all of these behaviors by management during a union organization campaign.

more employees speaking to each other about work-related issues such as safety concerns. Concerted activity may also apply to one employee if that employee is acting on behalf of a group of employees: raising complaints on their behalf or trying to coordinate a group action.

The effects of the NLRA were changed substantially when the **Labor Management Relations Act (LMRA)** was passed in 1947. Also known as the **Taft-Hartley Act**, the LMRA outlawed closed shops, jurisdictional strikes, and secondary boycotts. Taft-Hartley also established mechanisms to decertify unions. It permitted anti-union legislation at the state level (e.g., right-to-work laws). Finally, Taft-Hartley prohibited unions and employers from contributing funds from their treasuries to candidates for federal office. According to the LMRA, management is not afforded union protection, and the unions seeking the services of the NLRB must file documents with the US Department of Labor.

While the NLRA and Taft-Hartley are the most well-known laws involving labor relations, a large amount of legislation can be accurately described as labor relations. Minimum-wage laws, fair-practice rules, wage theft laws, and legislation mandating danger pay are all examples of laws that were passed because of influence from organized labor.

Weingarten rights refer to the right of a union employee to have union representation during an interview if that employee is being investigated. This term stems from the 1975 court case ***NLRB v. Weingarten* (1975)** between the NLRB and J. Weingarten, Inc., which operated a chain of convenience stores. Weingarten had denied an employee her request to have her steward or other union representative accompany her during a disciplinary investigation. The court held that this was in violation of the NLRA and that a union employee has a right to a union steward to be present during investigatory interviews.

Union organizing is also subject to important legislation. In the 1992 case ***Lechmere, Inc. v. NLRB***, union organizers used a shopping plaza parking lot in front of a Connecticut retail store to contact store employees. However, the parking lot was partially owned by the store owner, and the union organizers were not employees. The store owner barred the organizers from the parking lot, and they were forced to use other, public areas to work. The union organizers alleged that the owner violated the NLRA by prohibiting them from the parking lot. Initially the NLRB ruled in favor of the union. But on appeal, the Supreme Court reversed the decision, concluding that an employer does not have to allow distribution of union literature by nonemployees on the employer's property. The exception is if the location of the business and employees' residences puts them beyond reasonable reach (e.g., a very rural area).

EXAMPLE

5. When was the National Labor Relations Act enacted?
    A) 1910
    B) 1929
    C) 1935
    D) 1950

Federal Labor Law

The **US Department of Labor (DOL)** is a federal agency that administers and enforces more than 180 federal laws. These mandates and the regulations that implement them apply to numerous employment contexts, including specific industries and sizes of companies. Employers must understand and comply with certain laws. Some of the following laws are also discussed in chapter 4, "Total Rewards."

HELPFUL HINT

The exam will test on federal law, not state or local laws.

Individual states (and sometimes localities) create and enforce their own laws related to the employment of workers. Employers should be aware of the employment laws in all states in which they conduct business and employment. The state's department of labor can be contacted for state-specific information about employment laws. Employment practices and policies should be consistent with all laws that affect the organization to remain compliant and to avoid penalties.

Wages and Hours

The **Fair Labor Standards Act (FLSA)** mandates standards for the payment of regular wages, overtime, and the employment of minors. The FLSA affects most private and public employers. Employers are required to pay covered employees (i.e., **nonexempt employees**) at least the federal minimum wage and overtime pay of one-and-one-half times the regular rate of pay (time and a half). Children under sixteen can only work certain hours, and children under eighteen cannot work in dangerous nonagricultural jobs. See chapter 4 for more details on the FLSA.

The FLSA was amended by the Equal Pay Act of 1963 (see chapter 3).

Employee wage garnishments are regulated under the **Consumer Credit Protection Act (CCPA)**. The CCPA protects employees from being fired due to garnishment and also limits the amount that can be deducted from an individual's paycheck.

DID YOU KNOW?

The prudent person rule applies to ERISA, meaning that trustees must administer retirement plans prudently. Administrators should act only in the interest of plan beneficiaries, focusing on the decision-making process of plan administration

The **Employee Retirement Income Security Act (ERISA)** regulates employers who offer pension or welfare benefit plans to their employees. The act mandates a wide range of fiduciary, disclosure, and reporting requirements for plan fiduciaries and administrators; these provisions preempt many similar state laws. Under Title IV of ERISA, certain employers and plan administrators must fund an insurance system to protect specific kinds of retirement benefits, with premiums paid to the federal government's Pension Benefit Guaranty Corporation (PBGC).

Employees are entitled to sue for retroactive wage discrimination under the **Lilly Ledbetter Fair Pay Act**, which President Barack Obama signed into law in 2009. This law overturned a previous Supreme Court decision, *Ledbetter v. Goodyear Tire and Rubber Co.* (2007), which limited a person's ability to retroactively file a claim for compensation discrimination. According to the Lilly Ledbetter Fair Pay Act, each paycheck resets the 180-day statute of limitations for filing a lawsuit in regard to pay.

Since the Lilly Ledbetter Fair Pay Act was passed, an employee who started five, ten, or twenty years ago can file a complaint of discrimination based on their starting wages or other related instances that happened earlier in their career. Therefore, it is important that employers keep records of pay decisions.

EXAMPLES

6. Which law governs the number of hours that children may work?

- **A)** FMLA
- **B)** ADEA
- **C)** FLSA
- **D)** IRCA

7. If a nonexempt employee is off for Memorial Day but works ten hours a day the rest of the week, how many hours of overtime pay is she entitled to under the FLSA?

- **A)** zero
- **B)** eight
- **C)** forty
- **D)** forty-eight

Health, Welfare, and Workplace Safety

The **Patient Protection and Affordable Care Act (PPACA)** requires certain employers to offer affordable health insurance that provides minimum value to their full-time employees (and their dependents), to communicate about health care marketplaces to employees, and to provide a standardized summary of coverage to employees (among other requirements). It also requires insurers to cover preexisting conditions and to cover all insurance applicants. (Check with the US Department of Health and Human Services for the most current information on the PPACA.)

The **Consolidated Omnibus Budget Reconciliation Act (COBRA)** grants employees the right to keep the group health insurance (and pay the premium along with administrative costs) that they would otherwise lose after they quit or lose their jobs, or reduce their work hours. Most people can retain their insurance coverage for up to eighteen months (and longer in some situations). The **Health Insurance Portability and Accountability Act of 1996 (HIPAA)** provides opportunities for people to retain (or obtain) health insurance during qualifying events, protects the confidentiality and security of health care information, and provides mechanisms to control administrative costs.

The **Family and Medical Leave Act (FMLA)** provides up to twelve weeks of job-protected, unpaid leave during any twelve-month period to eligible, covered employees for the following reasons:

1. birth and care of the eligible employee's child, or placement for adoption or foster care of a child with the employee; or

2. care of an immediate family member (spouse, child, parent) who has a serious health condition; or

3. care of the employee's own serious health condition.

Eligible employees must be employed by an employer with at least fifty individuals in a 75-mile radius. The employee must have worked at the organization for at least twelve months and must have worked a minimum of 1,250 hours in the previous twelve months.

The law also requires that the employee's group health benefits be maintained during the leave. The FMLA was amended in 2008 to provide protections specifically for military families. Eligible, covered employees receive up to twenty-six weeks of military caregiver leave (to care for injured family members), and up to twelve weeks of qualifying exigency leave (to tend to matters related to deployment). These leaves are also unpaid; however, the employee's group health benefits must be maintained during the leave.

The **Occupational Safety and Health Act** also regulates the safety and health of employees; it is administered by the **Occupational Safety and Health Administration (OSHA)**, which may conduct inspections and investigations. Employers covered by the act must comply with the regulations and the safety and health standards established by OSHA.

Employers must also provide their employees with a work environment free from recognized, serious hazards. OSHA violations range from de minimus (the least serious) to willful (the most serious). A **de minimus violation** is a technical violation that has no direct impact on health or safety. A **willful violation** is an intentional violation or one that shows disregard for employee health or safety.

Some states operate under an OSHA State Plan whereby the state, rather than federal OSHA, protects employees and works to prevent work-related injuries, illnesses, and deaths. These plans must be at least as effective as federal OSHA and are monitored by OSHA.

EXAMPLE

8. The FMLA requires that an organization have how many employees in order to provide job-protected leave to qualified employees?

    A) 10
    B) 25
    C) 50
    D) 100

Special Requirements for Government Contractors

Companies that receive government contracts, grants, or financial aid must adhere to certain standards when it comes to wages, benefits, and safety and health standards.

- The **Davis-Bacon Act** requires the payment of prevailing wages and benefits to employees of contractors working on federal government construction projects.

- The **McNamara-O'Hara Service Contract Act** establishes wage rates and other work standards for employees of contractors providing services to the federal government.
- The **Walsh-Healey Public Contracts Act** requires the payment of minimum wages and other work standards by contractors providing materials and goods to the federal government.

Government contractors are also required to comply with federal affirmative action and equal opportunity laws, executive orders, and regulations. The **Office of Federal Contract Compliance Programs (OFCCP)** administers and enforces these laws. See chapter 3, "Workforce Planning and Management," for more information on affirmative action and the OFCCP.

Finally, the **Drug-Free Workplace Act of 1988** requires large federal contractors and grantees to have a drug-free workplace policy in place. At a minimum, these policies must prohibit the use, distribution, and manufacturing of controlled substances in the workplace. The act was designed to encourage a safe, drug-free workforce.

Industry-Specific Laws and Regulations

Several federal laws and regulations affect employers in the construction, agricultural, and mining industries.

- OSHA is in charge of specific safety and health regulations for employers in the construction industry.
- The **Migrant and Seasonal Agricultural Worker Protection Act (MSPA)** regulates the employment of agricultural workers.
- The **Fair Labor Standards Act (FLSA)** exempts agricultural workers from overtime premium pay but requires minimum wage for workers employed on larger farms. It also prohibits children under sixteen from working during school hours and in certain jobs deemed too dangerous.
- The **Federal Mine Safety and Health Act of 1977 (Mine Act)** mandates the safety and health standards of miners and the training of miners, levies penalties for violations, and allows inspectors to close dangerous mines.

EXAMPLE

9. What is the main purpose of the Davis-Bacon Act of 1931?
    - **A)** It requires federal contractors to implement affirmative action plans.
    - **B)** It prohibits discrimination on the basis of age of those over fifty.
    - **C)** It requires certain federal contractors to pay a prevailing wage to employees.
    - **D)** It requires the payment of overtime to nonexempt employees.

Other Federal Laws and Protections

Under the **Uniformed Services Employment and Reemployment Rights Act (USERRA)**, certain employees who serve in the armed forces have a right to reemployment with the employer they were employed with when they entered service, including reserves and National Guard.

The **Employee Polygraph Protection Act** prohibits most employers from using polygraphs (lie detectors) on employees. The law permits polygraph tests only in limited circumstances and prohibits employers from discharging, disciplining, or discriminating against employees or candidates for refusing to take the test. This act does not apply to federal, state, or local governments or to organizations that are contracted through the federal government to provide security.

Mass layoffs or plant closings may be subject to the **Worker Adjustment and Retraining Notification Act (WARN)**. WARN requires that employees receive at least a sixty-day warning of impending mass layoffs or plant closings. The WARN Act applies to businesses with over 100 employees who are laying off 33 percent of the workforce and at least fifty employees total.

Finally, many labor, public safety, and environmental laws protect **whistleblowers**—employees who make good-faith complaints about violations of the law committed by their employers. Penalties for violating these protections can include job reinstatement and payment of back wages. OSHA generally enforces whistleblower protections.

EXAMPLE

10. An applicant applying for which of the following positions may be required to take a polygraph test?
    - A) a teacher working with small children
    - B) a cashier at a grocery store
    - C) an agent at an insurance company
    - D) a police officer in a rural area

Company Policies and Culture

Managers and HR may refer to company policies when resolving disputes, disciplining employees, or addressing grievances. Policies should be outlined in the employee handbook, which should be available to all employees. **Organizational culture** refers to the organization's internal identity and how it is perceived. It is the shared values and beliefs that set norms and govern actions. This is not as rigid as a handbook or policies, but an organization's culture may factor in motivating employees.

An **employee handbook**, also referred to as an employee manual, is a documentation of the organization's policies and procedures that affect all employees. It can provide both employment and practical information like company rules, performance expectations, and office operations. A written employee handbook provides employees with clear guidance, explains organizational expectations, and fosters a culture in which problems are addressed fairly and consistently. It also outlines the organization's legal obligations as an employer and employee rights.

The **psychological contract** refers to these unwritten, informal expectations that exist between an employee and the organization where they work. These might be the expectation that an employee will get a raise every year or attend an annual professional conference.

Sections and Policies in Handbooks

Employee handbooks are an important tool for maintaining sound employee relations through the consistent and fair treatment of employees; they also provide clear, written expectations. Handbooks and written policies are a key method to documenting expectations and practices such as fair hiring and equal employment opportunity.

- **General Employment Information**: An employee handbook should provide an overview of the business and its general employment policies, including employment eligibility, job classifications, employee records, probationary periods, performance reviews, termination procedures, company transfers, and union information, if applicable.
- **Anti-discrimination Policies**: The handbook should contain information about the company's compliance with equal opportunity, anti-harassment, nondiscrimination, and disability laws; it should also include procedures for complaints and grievances.
- **Standards of Conduct** clarify expectations of employee conduct, including dress code and workplace behavior.
- **Conflict of Interest Statements** help protect the company's trade secrets and proprietary information.
- **Payroll Procedures** outline pay schedules, timekeeping requirements, overtime pay, salary increases, bonuses, and deductions for taxes and benefit premiums.
- **Work Schedules**: The handbook should explain work hours and schedules, attendance policies, punctuality, and reporting absences.
- **Safety and Security**: This section explains an employee's rights and obligations in ensuring a safe and secure workplace; it provides instructions on reporting accidents, injuries, and safety hazards. It also provides guidance on securing files, computers, and other company resources.
- **Use of Computers and Technology**: This section explains the appropriate use of company-provided hardware and software, steps to keep data secure, and how to handle personal information. Typically, it reminds employees that the company owns the technology and may monitor and regulate its use.
- **Employee Benefits**: This section outlines any benefit programs and eligibility requirements, including all benefits that are required by law.

- **Time-Off Policies**: This section explains employee entitlement to vacation time, sick time, paid holidays, family and medical leave, jury duty, military leave, and voting; policies and compliance with the law should be clearly documented.

Many handbooks also contain specific language that invokes the doctrine of **employment-at-will**. An employment-at-will statement specifies that an employee or employer may terminate the employment relationship, with or without reason, and with or without notice. In an at-will employment situation (which is the case in many states), there is no expectation of employment either indefinitely or for a specified duration.

As part of the onboarding process, new employees usually sign an acknowledgment form stating they have read and understand the information in the handbook. The company may need to update the handbook to reflect new policies, practices, and laws. Revisions should be communicated and distributed to employees and may require a new signed acknowledgment. Additionally, there may be different versions of the employee handbook for certain business units, subsidiaries, or locations. It is important to ensure that all versions are kept up to date.

Handbooks can be a useful tool in situations when corrective action needs to be taken with an employee, including termination of employment. When disciplining or terminating employees, it is helpful to refer to the specific policy or policies being violated. Doing so not only makes it clear to the employee that corrective action has been taken for an objective reason (e.g., violating an established policy); it also provides a reference enabling the company to better defend itself in litigation or complaints to governmental agencies. For this reason, a qualified employment attorney should review the company's handbook for compliance with the law and provide counsel as needed. See below for more information on employee discipline and termination.

Organizational Culture

Organizational culture is the workplace environment fostered by both leadership and employees. It describes how people within the organization interact with one another. Culture is affected by the experiences, personalities, values, beliefs, and principles of leadership and employees. Everyone within the organization contributes to the organizational culture in some way, and every organization has its own unique culture. Culture is often a reason why employees decide to remain at or leave an organization; it can also affect the organization's success.

An organization's culture affects its overall identity—the way that employees, clients, and the general public perceive it. For this reason, many organizations take great care to articulate and instill their values in everything they do; by developing a strong reputation, an organization attracts strong candidates for employment and reliable clients to purchase its products or services.

A shared organizational culture also helps to keep the workforce cohesive, especially when many employees come from different backgrounds, geographies, and cultures. Employees who feel supported by a sense of cultural unity and values are more likely to communicate effectively, work more collaboratively, and experience less conflict in the workplace.

Organizational culture is also a motivational tool. When employees feel connected to the organization and understand the significance of their role in it, they are more likely to feel invested in the organization's success. When they feel they have a stake in the success of the organization, they are more likely to work harder to accomplish the organization's goals. Having clear expectations and objectives set by management can help each employee understand his or her roles and responsibilities. This strategic management, combined with a system of recognition and feedback, helps keep employees aligned with the objectives of the business unit and organization. Employees will perform at their personal best to earn recognition and appreciation from management, and the organization will benefit from greater productivity and cooperation.

EXAMPLE

11. Which of the following laws allows certain employers to establish drug-testing policies?

- **A)** Occupational Safety and Health Act
- **B)** Drug-Free Workplace Act
- **C)** Worker Adjustment and Retraining Notification Act
- **D)** Drug Testing Act

Dispute Resolution

A major activity for HR professionals in employee relations is managing and resolving employee complaints and grievances. Complaints are generally less serious or severe than grievances, but both require timely and thoughtful action.

When an employee complains about work conditions or supervision, HR may actively investigate the situation, interview witnesses, and make recommendations for appropriate action. Management or HR may need to interpret a policy when situations are not expressly documented. They may recommend or take action based on the facts and whether policy applies to the situation.

In serious situations such as sexual harassment or discrimination, employees are typically reminded of their grievance and appeal rights, as well as any whistleblower protections. These situations are often documented in the employee's file or another record repository for future reference or required government reporting.

Complaints

Employee **complaints** are concerns or problems employees raise with human resources or management. Complaints may be minor, concerning issues like office supplies or coffee, or major, like a boss's management style. Some complaints are quickly and easily resolved by management or HR, while other complaints require more time, effort, and patience. Employee complaints can provide HR and management with useful information. They alert management to a problem before it grows out of control, and they give management a chance to respond and display commitment to addressing employee concerns.

When a manager or HR professional is presented with a complaint, he or she should listen carefully and openly to identify the concern behind the complaint. Asking pointed questions to gather facts will help to determine a proper plan of action. If other employees share the concern, obtaining their perspective will help to detect widespread problems. During this process, it is important to acknowledge the problem and clarify the action being taken. If action is not being taken on the complaint, it is appropriate to explain why. Demonstrating follow-through is essential to maintaining employee trust.

Employee complaints are inevitable, but methods exist to reduce them. HR professionals can encourage managers to give ongoing feedback on performance and to set clear expectations for the role. Employees can be encouraged to provide input on their work and on specific topics.

Not every employee is going to be satisfied with every action taken in an organization, but it is important not to penalize legitimate complainants—such an action could silence a valuable source of information. On the other hand, if an employee makes petty complaints on a regular basis, it is essential to have a frank conversation as to how these complaints are harming the organization's morale (if they are) and explain that the manner of the complaints is unacceptable.

Alternative Dispute Resolution

Alternative dispute resolution (ADR) refers to a number of tools that can be used to avoid litigation. ADRs can be any procedure or determination method that the parties have agreed on. The most common forms of ADR are arbitration and mediation. In **arbitration**, a neutral third party hears the evidence and decides on the outcome. (Arbitration is discussed above in union contexts but may also be used in nonunion contexts.) **Mediation** also uses a third party, but rather than making a final decision, the mediator helps negotiate the issue. In mediation, a decision or outcome is not reached unless both of the parties agree.

Grievances

When employees believe that a company policy, collective bargaining agreement, or law has been violated, they may make a formal complaint called a **grievance**. Grievances require immediate attention. A prompt response that results in a quick resolution of the grievance will improve employee morale and productivity, and can potentially prevent costly legal action.

It is imperative to take all grievances seriously, even if they may not seem valid. Grievance submission will follow either company protocol or bargaining unit contract language regarding whom to submit the grievance to, the timing around the grievance, and how the resolution is decided. HR can test the validity of a grievance by obtaining all relevant facts, as follows:

1. Actively listen to the person with the grievance. Ask follow-up questions and get concrete examples, dates, times, witnesses, and other alleged facts.
2. Consult with an employment attorney or union steward. It is important to take careful steps when validating a grievance. In unionized environments, the collective bargaining agreement may outline specific steps.
3. Interview potential witnesses, as appropriate, to get their perspective on the situation.
4. Provide an update to the person who submitted the grievance. If it seems that there is a problem that needs further investigation or action, specify what will be done. If the grievance does not seem valid, explain what was done up to this point, and why no further action will be taken.
5. If it is valid, take action to rectify the situation.

To take action on grievances:

1. If the organization has a collective bargaining agreement, follow the guidelines within it for handling grievances (and with the assistance of a union steward. Otherwise, refer to the employee handbook if there is a specific policy or procedure outlined.
2. Complainants and their supervisors should try to resolve the problem through discussion, which may be facilitated by HR.
3. If no resolution is met, the next higher level of management may speak with the employee, without repercussions. Again, this may also be facilitated by HR.
4. During any part of this process, HR may take a more active approach as a mediator. In some cases, however, a third-party arbitrator (outside of the organization) may be used.

There are steps an organization can take to minimize its risk of employee grievances. It is important to maintain a dialogue with employees and be open to feedback. A system should exist for employees to file legitimate complaints before they become bigger and unmanageable. Having a clear policy on submitting grievances, and detailing how the employer will handle grievances, will promote open communication. When employees complain, it is important not to retaliate. While not every complaint may be acted on, it is important to acknowledge the concerns and feelings of employees and to clearly communicate what action will or will not be taken and why.

EXAMPLES

12. What is the main purpose of a grievance procedure?
    A) to resolve conflict
    B) to empower employees to go on strike
    C) to terminate employees
    D) to provide progressive discipline

13. If an employee files a grievance, who typically handles it first?
- A) the employee's supervisor
- B) the company president or CEO
- C) a third party or arbitrator
- D) the union steward

Employee Discipline and Terminations

Most employees strive to do well at their jobs. Unfortunately, sometimes employees do not meet the expectations of the job, or they exhibit unacceptable behaviors. In such cases, most managers use **progressive discipline**, a series of steps that offers the employee opportunities to improve. If the employee does not improve during one step, then he or she progresses to the next step, which is considered more severe and moves closer to termination.

Managers or departments may have their own specific procedures and expectations aligned with those of the organization and clearly communicated to the employee. When employees perform poorly or behave unacceptably, the manager will identify the issues, counsel the employee, and discuss a plan to correct the problem.

Common examples of poor performance requiring counseling or discipline include **tardiness** (chronic lateness), **absenteeism** (failure to be at work during their scheduled time), poor performance, and general **misconduct** (unprofessional behavior).

By proactively identifying issues and being responsive to complaints or problems, organizations can stop or reduce disruptive behavior.

The Steps of Progressive Discipline

The number and details of each step in a **progressive discipline program** vary from employer to employer. Some employers, especially those subject to collective bargaining agreements, must strictly follow the order of each step in progressive discipline. Others reserve the right to use any or all steps necessary to address a particular issue. For example, an employee who does not follow the company's dress code may get a verbal warning, but physical violence toward another employee will likely result in immediate termination.

Taking the steps of progressive discipline is generally useful for repetitive, nonserious offenses (e.g., tardiness) or when there is no indication of the employee's improvement. Below are typical steps found in a progressive discipline procedure.

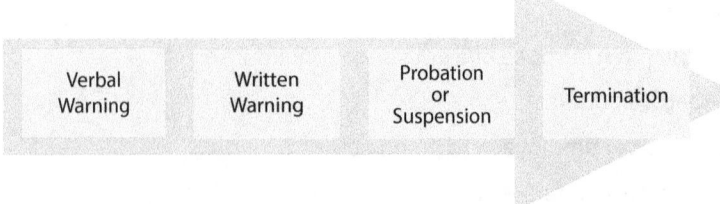

Figure 5.1. A Typical Progressive Discipline Procedure

A **verbal warning** is the least serious consequence of a poor behavior. It involves a conversation between a supervisor and an employee in which the inappropriate behavior is identified and expectations for improvement are made clear.

A **written warning** is appropriate when the employee ignores a verbal warning about their behavior or does not show improvement. The written warning, or "write-up," documents the incident, explains why the behavior is inappropriate (and references applicable company policies), explains what changes are expected, and describes the consequences of the continued behavior. Typically, an employee is asked to sign a copy to acknowledge receipt, although a signature may not necessarily mean the employee agrees with the contents of the write-up.

A **performance improvement plan** places the employee on **probation** and requires specific actions to be taken in order to meet the supervisor's expectations. The employee is required to follow the plan and to show improvement as a condition of continued employment.

Suspension

A **suspension** is often the final step before termination. A suspension lasts a certain duration. It may be paid or unpaid. Suspensions are accompanied by a document that outlines the terms of the suspension, specific steps to correct the issue, and the consequences for not improving. When the employee completes the suspension, the employee typically receives one last chance to demonstrate improvement.

Termination

The final step in the progressive discipline process, when behavioral problems are continual or the employee commits a serious offense like theft or violence, is the involuntary **termination** of employment known as **firing**. Usually a firing is immediate, but it should not be a surprise if the employer has clearly conveyed expectations and provided ongoing feedback to the employee.

There are other steps for progressive discipline that may be used, including demotions, temporary pay cuts, reassignments, and required training. Whatever methods are used, they should fit the behavior and resolve the problem rather than simply provide a route toward termination. Being open and frank during each step of the process can help the employee improve.

EXAMPLE

14. Progressive discipline is
    A) a "zero tolerance" policy.
    B) a system of discrimination in disciplining employees.
    C) a series of increasingly serious disciplinary actions.
    D) required under the FLSA.

Global Employee Relations

Many organizations operate in a global environment where employment issues, employment laws, and business practices can vary dramatically from country to country. HR professionals working in multinational companies must have a global perspective and a solid grasp of international employment issues to help the organization run smoothly. For multinational employers, there are unique employee relations issues to manage. Employees abroad may have unique health and safety issues due to political or economic conditions, regulations, or the physical environment. Additionally, the employer must also comply with the laws of the countries in which it operates.

Understanding Variations in Global Employment Law

Employment laws around the globe can vary greatly from country to country and region to region. It is critical, when operating on a worldwide basis, that the local employment laws be understood and executed. For instance, in some parts of the world, employees operate under contracts, and at-will employment is not recognized; other countries require paid leave or housing. Assuming employment law will be the same can lead to liability issues along with employee morale issues.

Global Health and Safety

Addressing safety and health issues is an important HR function. Employees working abroad may not enjoy the same quality of health care or environmental safety as those working in the United States. HR practitioners develop policies and employment benefits to support these employees. For example, companies may offer private insurance plans or funds for medical assistance to protect the health of employees. However, policies must comply with the country's laws and should be a generally accepted business practice in that country.

Depending on the regions in which they operate, international organizations may also have to address kidnapping, harassment, extortion, and other violence in regions experiencing political unrest. These dangers can occur either on or near the worksite or in residential areas. To protect employees working in dangerous areas, many firms provide bodyguards, change travel routes to make it difficult for criminals to track an individual, and provide safety training for family members of employees. Some companies may secure the grounds of their facilities with fences, barricades, armed guards, metal detectors, and/or surveillance devices. Others may take steps to minimize the visibility of the company.

To ensure the safety of expatriates (i.e., foreign nationals working abroad, the company may provide emergency protective services through an organization that can refer the ill or injured employee to adequate medical care if available locally, dispatch physicians, or transport employees to safety via aircraft. Additional safeguards may include in-country legal counsel or emergency cash for medical expenses or travel home.

Cultural Differences in the Workplace

Cultural norms in a country or region influence how people act and interact with one another. When employing international workers, the organization should be clear about its expectations of all its workers, regardless of geography. At the same time, in order to sustain successful operations in a country, an employer should understand the norms, values, and attitudes of the workers there.

If the organization's values contrast with the local culture, conflict may arise if the situation is not properly managed. Providing flexibility for certain cultural practices and helping employees assimilate into the organization can alleviate tensions.

Cultural differences among international employees may include different attitudes toward work. HR practitioners and management must recognize these differences and understand how they affect intra-company relations. HR practitioners can play a key role in facilitating open dialogue and providing learning opportunities for both US and non-US employees to work together more effectively. Examples include workshops and facilitated group discussion.

Global Labor Relations

The impact and nature of labor unions vary worldwide. In some locales, unions are weak or do not exist at all. Elsewhere, unions are extremely strong and may be closely aligned with political parties—Europe is one example. In other places, like the United States, unions have declined in influence and membership over time.

These differences affect how collective bargaining occurs too. In the United States, independent unions bargain with the employer over working conditions and wages. In Europe, however, bargaining is typically done industry-wide or regionally. Some countries require that companies have union representatives on their boards of directors (a practice called co-determination). It is important for multinational organizations to understand the norms of a country and be prepared to work with organized labor where it is present, in the manner that is customary for that country or region.

EXAMPLE

15. Americans working for an American company in Germany are referred to as
    - A) host country nationals.
    - B) external immigrants.
    - C) expatriates.
    - D) undocumented workers.

Answer Key

1. **A)** Collective bargaining is key to labor relations. A labor union's greatest strength is in its bargaining power.

2. **B)** Generally, if a company wants to change the terms of a collective bargaining agreement while it is in effect, it must give sixty days' notice.

3. **B)** Union-shop security clauses mean workers are required to join a union.

4. **D)** Right-to-work laws prohibit or limit union agreements that require employees' membership, or payment of union dues or fees, as a condition of employment. In short, they prohibit or limit union shops.

5. **C)** The National Labor Relations Act, or Wagner Act, was enacted in 1935.

6. **C)** The Fair Labor Standards Act (FLSA) mandates standards for the employment of minors, in addition to the payment of regular wages and overtime.

7. **A)** Nonexempt employees are not entitled to overtime pay under FLSA.

8. **C)** Companies with fifty or more employees in a 75-mile radius qualify for this FMLA provision.

9. **C)** The Davis-Bacon Act of 1931 requires the payment of prevailing wages and benefits to employees of contractors working on federal government construction projects.

10. **D)** The Employee Polygraph Protection Act does not apply to federal, state, or local governments or to organizations contracted through the federal government to provide security.

11. **B)** According to the Drug-Free Workplace Act, recipients of federal grants and some federal contractors must provide a drug-free workplace.

12. **A)** The main purpose of a grievance procedure is to resolve a conflict or dispute.

13. **A)** Not all employees are union members. Typically, a grievance is first addressed by an employee's supervisor. Depending on the situation, the grievance may progress higher in the organization, or to arbitration.

14. **C)** Progressive discipline is a series of steps that offers the employee opportunities to improve.

15. **C)** Individuals working in a country that is not their home country are called expatriates.

6 Learning, Development, and Evaluation

HR professionals are key to employee learning, training, and career growth. HR develops tools, processes, and structures for managers and employees to use in the growth and development of personnel. The HR function also requires understanding and analyzing data. This chapter explores learning styles, employee feedback, and critically evaluating information.

Training and Learning

Encouraging ongoing training and learning among employees is a key function of HR. HR professionals need an understanding of learning styles and theories to support their efforts in planning, developing, and implementing training programs.

A **learning organization** is one where employee development, learning, and training are part of the culture. Employees receive the opportunity and are also encouraged to continue their learning throughout their careers.

Career management, or **career development**, is the process of encouraging and enabling employees to understand, plan, and develop their career skills and interests. Career management does not just encourage employee growth; it ensures succession planning within the organization. An organization can foster career development in various ways: career counseling, mentoring programs, career development plans, and established training programs—either internal or external—made available to employees.

HELPFUL HINT

Managers coach and counsel employees; HR provides the tools for management to help employees grow. Developing employees is a team effort.

Adult Learning: Styles and Conditions for Learning

Adult learning styles refer to the method by which adults best absorb a new concept. Some people understand a message by seeing it. Others most effectively absorb a message by hearing it. Finally, still others learn by acting out a process or through another means.

To effectively communicate with staff, organizational leadership and human resources must be cognizant of adult learning styles:

- visual (spatial)—learning through pictures, drawings, and images
- aural (auditory-musical)—learning through sound or music
- verbal (linguistic)—learning through words (verbal and writing)
- physical (kinesthetic)—learning through touch or movement
- logical (mathematical)—learning through logic or reasoning

While it is not always practical to tailor a message or concept to every learning style, organizations should strive to use a combination of methods and media that are appropriate for the particular message and the available resources.

Adult learners have several distinct traits that HR and the organization should consider while developing learning and development programs. Adult learners are **independent** and **self-directed**. In training programs, employees should be actively engaged in the learning process. Adult learners are **results-oriented** and **practical**. These learners should receive information that they can apply immediately. Adult learners may be **resistant to change** and will require justification for new behaviors. Finally, adult learners may **learn more slowly** than younger learners. However, they may be more skilled at integrating new knowledge with previous experience.

Psychologist Benjamin Bloom described three domains of learning:

- The **cognitive domain** includes collecting, synthesizing, and applying knowledge.
- The **affective domain** involves emotions and attitudes, including the ability to be aware of emotions and to respond to them.
- The **psychomotor domain** relates to motor skills, including the ability to perform complex skills and to create new movement patterns.

DID YOU KNOW?

The knowledge, skills, and abilities (KSAs) align with the three learning domains: Knowledge is cognitive learning, skills are psychomotor learning, and abilities are affective learning.

Program design and implementation plans should address all three learning domains. For example, an employee who is learning about a new online filing system may need to be taught about the positive impacts of the new system (cognitive domain), how to manage negative emotions related to changing systems (affective domain), and how to correctly use the new system (psychomotor domain).

Motivation

A training program should assess learners' source of **motivation** in order to better educate, encourage, and advocate for them.

- **Intrinsic motivation** is the desire to achieve a goal, seek challenges, or complete a task that is driven by enjoyment and personal satisfaction. For instance, an employee who completes a training exercise because it is enjoyable or one who learns a skill they desired to know is intrinsically motivated.
- **Extrinsic motivation** is the desire to accomplish a goal that is driven by external factors like praise, financial rewards or other benefits, or

punishment. An employee who completes a training exercise to avoid a disciplinary action or to earn a bonus is extrinsically motivated.

An individual's **readiness to learn** can be shaped by many factors, including openness to new information, emotional response (e.g., denial, anxiety), and support systems. In the workplace, HR or management must review an individual's readiness to learn because it will impact their ability to learn and the success of the development program. Employees who are struggling with readiness to learn may need proactive steps to help them become open to the training or development. This may include creating time for training outside their normal routine, instilling motivation, or providing remedial training.

Training Programs and Techniques

Employee training programs are important for educating staff, preparing them to perform a job, and helping them acquire valuable skills that are relevant to the job. In other words, training helps employees acquire the tools, strategies, and techniques necessary to be successful at their jobs.

Through training and development programs, the organization can establish desired cultures and move toward long-term goals. HR plays a critical role in developing culture, and strategic initiatives that support cultural development should be incorporated into the training planning. Staff education should reinforce organizational values and ensure that those values are understood and practiced.

Furthermore, it is key to include diversity and equity training in personnel development to realize the benefits of a diverse workplace. Through education programs, awareness, organizational commitment, sensitivity, and valuing diversity can be reinforced and taught throughout the organization. Organizations benefit from the perspectives and contributions of employees of various backgrounds. Ensuring employees of every race, ethnicity, gender identity, sexual orientation, religion or lack of religion, ability or disability, and age are respected and treated fairly in the workplace is essential. Beyond the legal implications, a diverse workplace strengthens the organization, its product or service, and its workforce. Employees from different backgrounds can bring their perspectives to improve internal and external processes.

Training methods fall into two main categories: cognitive and behavioral.

Cognitive methods of training are based on theoretical training that focuses on processes, guidelines, methods, and rules. Information is provided either in verbal or written form and results in increased knowledge or change of mindset. Examples of cognitive-based training include:

- live demonstrations and tutorials
- lectures to provide information
- group discussions for process-based problem-solving
- computer or web-based training (eLearning)

Behavioral methods of training are interactive and intended to spark creative thinking. They focus on employee behaviors and problem-solving rather than processes. Examples of behavioral training include:

- role-playing with open-ended problem-solving
- behavior modeling to compare scenarios
- case studies with open discussion about outcomes
- group brainstorming to solve sample problems

Cognitive training can be useful for providing consistency; however, it does not encourage creative thinking. Behavioral methods challenge trainees to develop their own solutions, but they do not offer uniformity. The organization should account for the advantages and disadvantages of each method and the desired outcome of training when determining which type of training to use. In addition, although these two methods of training are the most commonly used, other effective training methods include one-on-one coaching and mentoring, soft skills training, and formal and informal feedback.

Program Design and Implementation

A critical part of any training and development program is the design. Without fully understanding the needs of an organization or individual, an educational program may have little impact and fail to deliver the return on investment that was desired. HR must understand the strategic needs of an organization and carefully analyze the performance gaps. By completing this step, the programs can be strategically designed to reinforce strategic initiatives and build the necessary skills of the workforce moving forward.

When designing a training program, the principles of adult learning, learning styles, and training techniques that were discussed previously must be incorporated. One tool that can be used for program design and implementation is the **ADDIE model**, which stands for analysis, design, development, implementation, and evaluation.

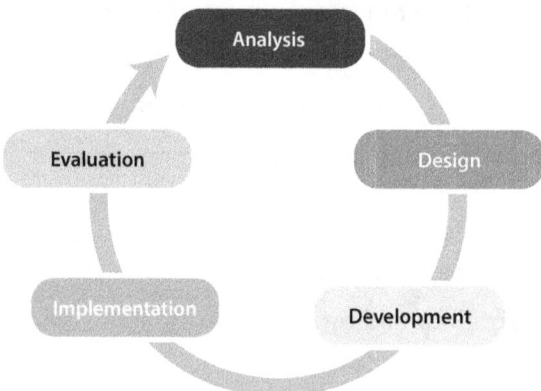

Figure 6.1. The ADDIE Model

During the analysis phase, the designer will consider the desired new behaviors, delivery options, who will participate, the participants' abilities and skills, and the timeline of the project. An **individual development plan (IDP)** can be one source to identify individuals' needs. An IDP is a commitment between an employee and supervisor that identifies the employee's growth opportunities and development needs.

The designer might also use a **training needs assessment** to identify the training requirements and skill levels throughout the organization during the analysis phase of the ADDIE model. By looking at the gap between the needs and the actual abilities, the designer can identify the causes and reasons for these gaps. By taking this step, the instruction can focus on the right personnel, prioritize the training needs, engage the staff by showing the gap and ROI of the training, and identify tools and methods to be used within the training itself. A training needs assessment can focus on the organization as a whole, specific roles within the organization, and/or on the individual personnel.

After the designer completes the assessment phase, they will move on to the design phase, where specific content, methods, and goals are identified. Training can be delivered in-person within a traditional lecture or classroom style, digital or technological resources also known as eLearning, on-the-job training, coaching and mentoring, job rotation or shadowing, or outside programming or classes.

Each of these methods has advantages and disadvantages that should be assessed for the specific training needs. eLearning is flexible and can often be accessed at any time, can be given over a large region or group of employees, and can be cost-effective. However, it often limits the participants' ability to interact with an instructor or allow more modified content. Additionally, employees who lack time-management skills might struggle with self-paced courses.

When designing training, it is important to remember the 70-20-10 model of learning. This model says that 70 percent of learning happens through doing, 20 percent happens by coaching or mentoring from others, and 10 percent happens through formal learning. By using this type of model and the principles of adult learning, it is important to design a program that incorporates multiple methods.

After the ADDIE design phase, the designer moves into the development phase, where the actual content and course materials are created. The construction of these items should only happen after assessment and design are completed. If using an outside resource or platform, the same holds true. Selection should happen only after the first two phases are completed and the needs are fully understood.

The ADDIE implementation phase is when the instructor preps and delivers that actual course material. At this point the training should be set up for success; however, it is important to always include the last ADDIE phase—evaluation—so that any training can be improved upon and issues can be identified. During the evaluation, time should be spent developing specific questions that will allow the organization to determine the effectiveness of the education in reaching the established goals. This may include not only looking at the participants' reaction to the training but also at the learning, changes in work, and the overall results.

One model that can be used for the ADDIE evaluation phase is **Kirkpatrick's Four Levels of Learning Evaluation**, which allows effective evaluation of training programs. Historically, most organizations only focus on reaction, or level one of Kirkpatrick's model. However, reaction only measures how participants felt about and during the training. Kirkpatrick's Four Levels of Learning Evaluation looks deeper at not only the participants' reaction but also how well they learned and whether this training will impact their future performance.

The four levels of this model are reaction, learning, behavior, and results:

1. Reaction: measures satisfaction with training, looking at how engaged learners were during the training and whether they felt the training was valuable. Questions might include: "Was the training worth your time?" "Did you like the location?" "Did you enjoy the activities?" "How will you use what you learned?"

2. Learning: degree to which participants' skills or knowledge increased due to training. This can be measured through evaluation that may include a before-and-after test to determine change.

3. Behavior: degree to which participants' behavior increased due to training and how they apply their new knowledge. This evaluation would take place weeks or months after the training, looking at if the trainees have used the new skills, if there has been a change in their behaviors, and/or if they have shared this new information with others within their team.

4. Results: results achieved due to training. Results looks at quantitative measurements such as improved productivity and quality of work. By looking at these results, a return on investment (ROI), for the training can be computed.

A **learning management system (LMS)** is an application that supports an organization's training and development activities. It facilitates online training, tracks and reports on employee progress, and maintains learning aids. An LMS intersects easily with **eLearning**, or online learning, which may be self-directed. Corporate training departments use LMS applications to deliver online training, to maintain electronic records, and to automate employee registration in training programs. An LMS system is often part of an overarching HRIS system.

EXAMPLES

1. What is employee training?
    - A) the development of skills that apply to an employee's job
    - B) teaching employees about their requirements
    - C) one-on-one tutoring
    - D) an intervention with employees who need special attention

2. Which of the following is an example of behavioral-based training?

   A) self-directed online learning

   B) live demonstrations

   C) case studies with open discussion

   D) tutorials

Employee Feedback and Performance Appraisals

Feedback is one of the most important duties of managers and is critical to an employee's success. HR practitioners have a key role in collaborating with management to ensure that feedback is timely, consistent, and impactful. Feedback can be formal (e.g., performance reviews, write-ups) or informal (e.g., conversations, meetings).

Feedback and appraisals can also affect an employee's compensation. **Performance management** measures an individual's performance, coaches and develops employees, and rewards and recognizes performance.

Informal Feedback

Informal feedback is instant, in-the-moment advice that occurs outside the formal performance review (which occurs typically once a year). Examples of informal feedback include praising an employee for accomplishing a goal, correcting a mistake, or providing **constructive criticism**. Feedback should be specific, should use data or examples, and should be immediate. Providing feedback can help effective employees sustain their success, and coach poor or average employees in taking immediate steps to improve. Managers can and should provide feedback to employees in the situations that follow.

Situations for positive reinforcement include when an employee:

- demonstrates improvement in a development area.
- goes "above and beyond," or exceeds, his or her job responsibilities.
- "pitches in," helping colleagues beyond the bounds of his or her job duties.
- reaches an important goal or milestone.
- sets a good example for others.

Situations for constructive criticism include when an employee:

- is not performing the job correctly and is making mistakes.
- is being disruptive to the team or not following rules.
- is not meeting the expectations of the job.
- needs to develop a particular skill.

Employees usually perform better when they receive timely and specific feedback from their managers. Sometimes employees are not aware that their performance is problematic. Or they may not be aware that they are exceeding expectations. Feedback provides them with specific information they need about the manager's expectations. Constructive feedback allows an employee to correct their behavior, and praise lets them know they should stay on the same path. When an employee's behavior changes, it is important for the manager to follow up and give new feedback as necessary.

Performance Appraisals

In addition to informal feedback, formal feedback is an important way to support the success of the organization's workforce. The most common type of formal feedback is the **performance appraisal**, or performance evaluation, which is a documented assessment of the employee's performance in a specific period of time (typically a year) that contributes to the employee's overall development.

Performance appraisals complement the organization's strategic plan, which determines individual job tasks and requirements. The appraisal is based on results achieved by the employee in his or her job. It measures skills and accomplishments with reasonable accuracy and uniformity, often using a predetermined **rating scale**, rubric, and criteria. The evaluation should be conducted using specific data, examples, and feedback from colleagues or customers. Done thoroughly, the appraisal identifies areas to improve performance and helps the employee to grow professionally.

Periodic reviews enable managers to stay aware of their employees' abilities, to set a clear path moving forward, and to help their teams work more effectively. Performance appraisals should recognize the employees' achievements, evaluate their progress, and identify ways to improve or expand their skills. If the manager has been providing ongoing and specific feedback during the year, the performance appraisal should not present many surprises to the employee. In these cases, the appraisal is a tool for documenting the employee's progress. Typically, the appraisal is signed by both the manager and employee to confirm receipt of the document and confirm the performance conversation.

Appraisals are also tools for managing organizational risk. Sometimes these documents are requested during litigation or hearings with governmental agencies (for unemployment or discrimination claims). Organizations that have thorough, timely, and relevant performance appraisals documented in the employee's file can respond to complaints more effectively. If an organization does not document performance appraisals, or if it carries out appraisals inconsistently, it places itself at risk. A licensed employment attorney can help employers understand their particular risk and respond to complaints if they arise.

One type of appraisal that has gained popularity is the **360 review**. With the 360-degree performance review, multiple sources are asked to contribute to an employee's evaluation. These could include coworkers, subordinates, and customers along with the supervisor and the employee themselves. The 360 review is a way to obtain a full picture of the employee's impact on the company.

Development needs analysis can help managers identify the needs of an individual. Types of development needs assessments include assessment centers, psychological testing, or performance appraisals. Assessment centers offer a

HELPFUL HINT

Ranking is a method used to compare employees' relative performance. A forced distribution method of rating employees ranks them in order of productivity.

collection of tests or exercises that determine an individual's skill and abilities around identified activities and tasks.

EXAMPLES

3. What is a performance evaluation also called?
   A) a performance appraisal
   B) a write-up
   C) progressive discipline
   D) informal feedback

4. Who typically provides feedback on an employee's performance in a 360-degree performance appraisal system?
   A) peers
   B) subordinates
   C) current supervisor
   D) all of the above

Critical Evaluation

Critical evaluation is key to the HR function. **Critical evaluation** means the HR professional understands how to analyze data and implement it to further the organization's objectives. As a strategic partner to the organization, HR must not only be able to collect data but also to analyze and use data in a predictive manner. HR must move from simply operational reporting, or simply looking at traditional data such as head count or attrition, and move to predictive analytics where HR data and analytics play a strategic part in organizational decision-making by using scenario planning and forecasting.

Being a Data Advocate

Senior-level HR understands the use of data to not only speak the language of business but also to predict future needs. There is a significant amount of data that can drive and inform decision-making.

Evidence-based decision-making involves making decisions around actual evidence, data, and root-cause analysis instead of using gut feeling or intuition. In this manner, decisions are based on facts rather than assumptions. In regard to employee development, training, and performance management, facts, rather than feelings, must drive the design and implantation of programs. In the ADDIE model discussed previously, the importance of the assessment phase to determine the actual needs of the organization and the individuals was examined.

HR professionals should be cautious of rater errors that could cloud their judgment in making decisions.

- The **halo effect** is when the interviewer allows one positive characteristic of a candidate to overly influence their decision.
- The **similar-to-me effect** happens when the rater allows characteristics they share with the employee to impact the rating.
- The **recency effect** occurs when the rater gives greater importance to recent events than to the overall performance of the employee or candidate.
- The **horns effect** happens when the rater allows one negative characteristic to influence the entire rating.
- **Central tendency** errors occur when a manager gives most or all employees a rating that falls in the middle of the scale.

Through evidence-based decision-making, HR is able to report key findings to leadership, to recommend courses of action, and to measure the return on investment.

Data Gathering and Analysis

Several techniques and methods exist for gathering data. It is important to understand the different data collection methods in order to choose the technique that will get the information needed.

Surveys are a quick, easy, and cost-effective method to gather data. A **survey** involves collecting information from a sample of the targeted group. Surveys can be done via a questionnaire or an interview. Data collected through the surveys is then used in tracking and determining a situation.

Similar to surveys, **focus groups** obtain information from individuals who represent a sample of a larger group. Typically, a focus group comprises six to twelve participants who participate in a discussion led by a facilitator. It is important that a focus group be led by a trained individual who knows how to pose questions in a manner that does not lead or influence the group members' responses.

Design of both the survey and focus groups are critical in obtaining objective information. Distortion of information is a risk if employees feel that their pay or position may be in jeopardy.

Measurement error refers to all the variations that impact a participant's performance. These variations might include conditions (e.g., quietness of the room, behavior of the facilitator or survey administrator) or the emotional state of the participant.

Though evidence-based decision-making and the use of HR data has obvious benefits, there still are **risks to the organization**. Even advanced technology, like artificial intelligence (AI), may be prone to inaccuracy and potentially unreliable in its predictions. Additionally, personal data must be protected and only shared appropriately. Breaches in a company's systems or unsecured databases may lead to private information being shared. It is critical that the business has a policy around record-keeping and how to protect employee information.

When collecting data, completing an environmental scan can provide insight into future planning by determining how external and internal factors could impact the business and personnel. **Environmental factors** could include internal organizational metrics, economic trends, competition for employees, political and legal trends, technological trends, social trends, or geographic trends like opening and closing of plants or offices in the area.

Another practice in human resources analytics is benchmarking. In **benchmarking**, an analyst compares such items as HR policies, practices, wages, and benefits with those of another organization. However, benchmarking can also happen within an organization in larger companies with multiple locations or divisions. Benchmarks and benchmark data are then used to measure HR initiatives in relationship to competitors and other relevant businesses. This way HR ensures best practices of its initiatives and programs.

In general, data and metrics are a way that HR can measure the success and outcome of an initiative. These strategies allow HR to measure the impact of an initiative upon an organization by analyzing trends within the data, which allows for an objective evaluation.

HR should understand basic statistical methods including descriptive statistics, correlations, and measurements such as reliability and validity. The term **descriptive statistics** means a brief, meaningful description, or basic summary, of a data set. This may include the distribution and spread of information, such as the range of wage data, or it might provide information about the mean or average, such as an average wage for a position. Summary of the data might include items such as the range, quartiles, deviation, and variance.

Correlation explains the relationship between two items or variables. For example, an HR practitioner might question whether there is a correlation between gender and wages. Correlation can be determined through tools like regression analysis or scatterplots.

> **HELPFUL HINT**
>
> A SWOT analysis looks at internal strengths and weaknesses and external opportunities and threats. A PESTLE analysis examines political, economic, social, technological, legal, and environmental factors. See chapter 1 for more information on SWOT and PESTLE analyses.

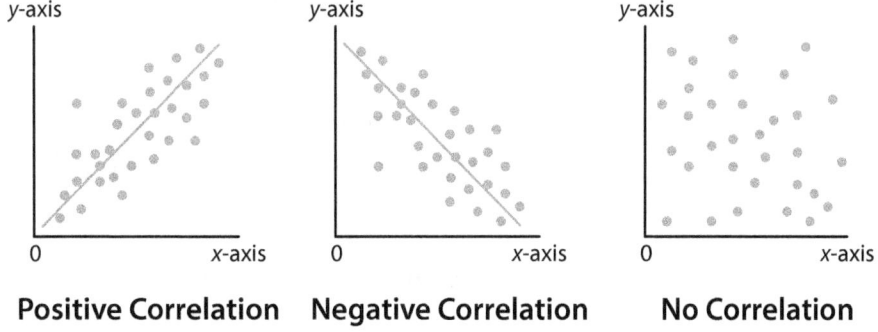

Figure 6.2. Scatterplots Showing Correlation

It is also important to understand if the data is reliable and valid. **Reliability** is the consistency of the measurement. Take, for example, a performance scoring system. To be reliable, the system must measure employees in the same manner. Though their scores may be different, *how* they are measured is consistent.

On the other hand, **validity** refers to what is being measured and whether it is relevant. In the example of a performance review, if an employee's performance on a nonwork-related issue is being measured, that item is not valid. It may be a reliable measurement, but it is it not accurate or relevant to the actual review.

When analyzing data, it is important to spot misleading or flawed data. Looking at validity and reliability is one way to do this, but it is also important to consider how the data is presented. For instance, what is the scale of the graph? Is it sized in a particular way to make a topic look more impactful than it actually is? What is the actual size of the data? Is a 25 percent increase due to the addition of five people to a twenty-person company? Or 500 to a 20,000-person company? Is the data complete, or have only specific periods of times or items been included? It is important to not accept data on face value but to objectively interpret it to ensure a full understanding of the information.

HR professionals ensure **objectivity in interpreting data** by using metrics and data. They make decisions based on facts, not emotion, opinion, or perception. Objectivity also allows HR to build a business case for decisions, goals, and strategies.

> **HELPFUL HINT**
>
> Think of the concept of reliability the same as you would a person who is reliable. A reliable person behaves as expected every time. A reliable assessment instrument does too.

HR Metrics

What kind of data do HR professionals study? **HR metrics** show important trends and information regarding the organization's personnel. This information helps decision-makers improve the organization and meet employees' needs. HR practitioners can track and analyze several metrics.

TABLE 6.1. Common HR Metrics

METRIC	CALCULATION
Cost per hire	$\dfrac{\text{recruitment costs}}{\text{(compensation cost + benefits cost)}}$
Average time to fill a position	$\dfrac{\text{sum of days to fill all jobs in a period}}{\text{total jobs filled in the period}}$
Absence rate	$\dfrac{\text{number of days absent in month for all employees}}{\text{(average number of employees during a month} \times \text{number of workdays)}}$
Benefit costs per employee	$\dfrac{\text{total cost of employee benefit or program}}{\text{total employees}}$
Benefit utilization rate	$\dfrac{\text{total number of employees using a benefit}}{\text{total number of employees eligible to use a benefit}}$

METRIC	CALCULATION
Average tenure	total service for all active employees / total number of active employees
Turnover (annual)	number of employees terminating during a twelve-month period / average number of employees during the same period
Turnover costs	total costs of separation + recruitment costs + lost productivity + training costs

Organizations can track and measure other calculations, depending on the organization's needs. When deciding which metrics to analyze and track, consider these factors:

- What metrics are important to organizational leaders and the strategic plan?
- What data must be obtained to calculate these metrics, and from what sources should they be obtained?
- How will data be analyzed, and against what sources will it be benchmarked?
- How can the analysis be presented for use in planning, development, and problem-solving?

EXAMPLES

5. Which of the following factors is considered in an environmental scan?
    A) competition
    B) succession plan
    C) staffing metrics
    D) compensation analysis

6. A group of employees all fill out a survey with the exact same answers, a surprising result. HR finds out later that the room in which the survey was administered was very hot; the AC was out of order, and employees were uncomfortable and eager to leave the room quickly. What can be said about this data?
    A) The data likely has a measurement error.
    B) The survey given was unreliable.
    C) The survey is not valid.
    D) It could be used for initial screening for a new product.

Answer Key

1. **A)** Employee training refers to helping an employee develop skills that apply to their job or career path.

2. **C)** A case study with open discussion would spark creative thinking and is an example of behavioral-based training.

3. **A)** A performance evaluation is a formal, documented assessment of an employee's performance in a given time period (usually a year). It is also called a performance appraisal.

4. **D)** In a 360-degree performance review, multiple sources are asked to contribute to an employee's evaluation. The employee may also contribute.

5. **A)** An organization's competition is an external factor in its operating environment. Competition would be examined in an environmental scan.

6. **A)** If employees were uncomfortable and wanted to leave quickly, it is unlikely they took the time to answer survey questions carefully and thoughtfully. The data probably contains a measurement error. Measurement error refers to the factors, such as test conditions, that impact the test results.

7 Risk Management

Risk is defined as the probability that a specific outcome (or harm) will occur. **Risk management** may deal not only with the health and safety of employees but also with such issues as business interruption or enterprise management; preventing and dealing with violence in the workplace and security measures, terrorism, and cybersecurity; and business continuity and emergency planning.

HR is involved in risk management on many levels. HR's role in risk management may include creating and disseminating a response plan, investigating an incident, purchasing insurance coverages, or offering support to an organization in the aftermath of an event.

Risk management differs from workplace safety. Safety focuses on reducing the risk of injury to the employee in the workplace, whereas risk management focuses on protecting the business and employees from external factors. A workplace security plan may include such issues as protecting intellectual property, developing crisis management plans, and taking steps to avoid theft and fraud. HR might work alone or directly with other parts of the organization such as finance, technology, or operations to create teams to work on these threats and devise actions to mitigate any future incidents.

Legal Compliance

Compliance means different things depending on the company or industry. However, all companies with employees must comply with federal and state employment laws. Many of these laws, such as the Fair Labor Standards Act and the Occupational Safety and Health Act (OSHA), have been described throughout this guide. It is the responsibility of employers to understand all the laws that apply to their business in the location(s) where they operate. Companies should develop sound, well-documented policies, and train employees to understand

and follow them. There should also be procedures for handling employees who do not comply with a company policy (and may therefore be noncompliant with the law).

Companies must also understand and follow regulations and case law. **Regulations** are specific directives with the same force of law enacted by federal agencies in order to execute acts of Congress. The Family and Medical Leave Act is an example of a law passed by Congress that resulted in regulations and procedures developed by the Department of Labor, the regulatory agency that implements the law. The Internal Revenue Service (IRS) also creates regulations that can affect employee payroll and benefits.

Case law, on the other hand, refers to laws that are based on judicial decisions that arise out of court cases involving legal issues such as regulations, established laws, or statutes.

The Federal Rulemaking Process

The **Administrative Procedure Act** outlines the method by which federal rules must be proposed, amended, and finalized. The basic steps for promulgating a federal rule or regulation follow. The Administrative Procedure Act, passed in 1946, was designed to govern the process that federal agencies must follow when developing and issuing new federal acts.

Figure 7.1. The Federal Rulemaking Process

The applicable law (which the regulation supports) specifies the process used to create accompanying regulations. Some regulations require only publication and an opportunity for comments to become final. Others require publication and formal public hearings. Once a regulation becomes "final rule" and takes effect, it is published in the Federal Register, the Code of Federal Regulations (CFR), and on the website of the regulatory agency. Companies then must ensure **regulatory compliance**; their policies and procedures must be in accordance with regulations.

EXAMPLES

1. What is the level of probability that an organization may be exposed to a hazard or loss?

    A) risk

    B) adverse impact

    C) vulnerability

    D) loss analysis

2. Which of the following BEST describes risk management?

    A) reducing the risk of workplace injury to employees

    B) limiting financial losses a company may face year over year

    C) adhering to regulations to ensure regulatory compliance

    D) safeguarding employees and the organization from external factors

3. Which of the following BEST defines federal regulations?

    A) sound, well-documented policies

    B) acts of Congress at the federal level

    C) laws based on judicial decisions that emerge from court cases

    D) directives that have the force of law enacted by federal agencies

Safety and Health

Organizations have a responsibility to protect the safety, health, and well-being of their employees. Ensuring safety and health is a moral obligation due to its humanitarian nature. At the same time, an employer has legal obligations to ensure employee safety and health; employers must follow specific guidelines under these laws and face certain penalties and fines if they do not. Taking the necessary precautions can also reduce costs the business may incur, including the costs of medical care, sick leave, disability benefits, and lost productivity.

Workplace Hazards

Depending on the nature of the business and where it conducts its operations, there are a number of health and safety hazards and risks that employees may face. A workplace **hazard** is something that can cause harm if it is not mitigated or eliminated. It is the role of HR professionals or safety professionals to identify hazards and assess risks that affect employees for the moral, legal, and financial reasons described previously.

In general, there are three categories of workplace hazards (described below): physical, health, and psychosocial. Some industries may be more prone to certain hazards than others. For example, the construction industry may have many physical hazards, whereas the financial industry may have many psychosocial hazards.

TABLE 7.1. Workplace Hazards

Physical hazards include:
- heavy machinery
- slippery surfaces
- hot temperature or surfaces
- confined spaces
- extreme heights

Health hazards include:
- chemical exposure
- bacteria
- mold
- blood-borne pathogens and other communicable diseases
- acids
- vapors
- fire and explosions
- repetitive trauma and ergonomics

Psychosocial hazards include:
- job insecurity
- poor work-life balance
- high demands
- long work hours
- unfair working conditions

HELPFUL HINT

Safety rules and procedures should be regularly evaluated for their effectiveness, with management and employee input.

HR, along with a safety officer in some organizations, can take measures to mitigate workplace hazards. HR professionals should develop methods and procedures to manage hazards that can cause injury to workers and facilities. Workspaces, equipment, procedures, and services should periodically be evaluated for safety. Employees should be actively included in developing safe working practices. Resources should be allocated to train employees on safety and to enforce safety rules.

OSHA has three levels of hazard mitigation or control that cannot be eliminated from the workplace. The first level includes **engineering controls**: the redesign of a machine or work area to remove the exposure to the employee. Engineering controls might mean installing guards, a railing, or barriers. The next level of hazard mitigation is **administrative controls**: job rotation or safety procedures that limit an employee's exposure. The final level is the use of **personal protective equipment (PPE)**. PPE should only be used when engineering or administrative controls are not possible in eliminating the hazard.

Effective safety officers, who might also have the role of HR, must be well versed in those laws and regulations that govern employee health and safety (such as the Organizational Safety and Health Act) as well as industry standards on best practices. They must be able to design operational procedures and recordkeeping systems for clarity and accountability. They should also be able to identify and implement the safety equipment and resources necessary to protect employees as they conduct their jobs.

Security

Just as a home needs to be secure from intruders, an organization also has **security** needs. A data breach, for example, can lead to key information being leaked to competitors and can harm the organization financially. An intruder breaking into the company's headquarters can steal important records, potentially resulting in financial or other losses. Protecting the physical security of the organization's employees, facilities, infrastructure, and resources is vital to its survival. An organization should carefully plan its security strategy.

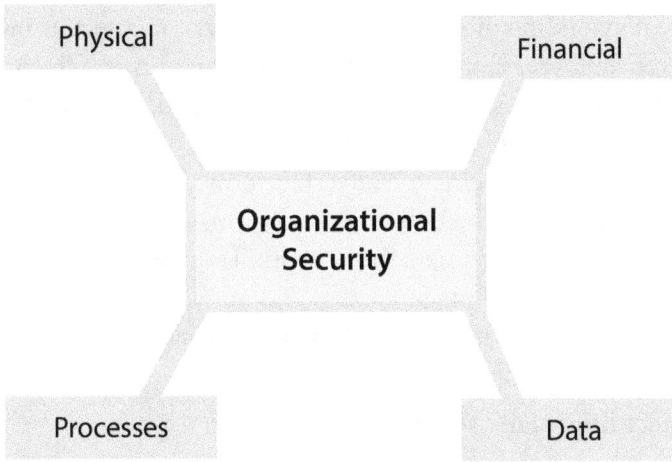

Figure 7.2. Components of Organizational Security

The following are essential steps in developing an organizational security policy.

1. **Develop security policies and procedures that are well documented and accessible to all employees.**

This documentation shows the organization's commitment to security and clarifies procedures to management, which enforces security concerns on a day-to-day basis.

2. **Maintain a physically secure environment.**

If the business is at risk of theft, robberies, violence, or other crimes, it is important to install surveillance and to secure entries, metal detectors, and other devices to monitor the premises and prevent security breaches. The organization should also have policies and procedures regarding employees' handling of company equipment, including computers. The policies should clearly indicate what steps the employee should take when company property is lost or stolen, so that the organization can respond appropriately and mitigate the effects of that loss.

3. **Restrict information only to those who need to know it.**

Employees should have access only to the files, records, and information necessary to conduct their jobs. In particular, access to sensitive information should be limited to those who need it to perform a certain function or who are in a position to make decisions related to that information. Additionally, the company should have a policy requiring employees to protect the confidentiality of any sensitive or proprietary information to which they have access. In some industries, it is important to have employees complete a noncompete and/or confidentiality agreement to ensure specific information is kept confidential even after an employee leaves the company.

4. **Protect data from loss, theft, or intrusion.**

Viruses, malware, and cyberattacks threaten an organization's technological infrastructure. The organization should install the appropriate firewalls, antivirus software, and network monitoring software necessary to protect its infrastructure from attacks. Employees should be required to maintain strong computer and network passwords; these passwords should be changed regularly. The organization should have "acceptable use" policies restricting employees from accessing suspicious websites (to minimize inadvertent downloads that can be harmful to their computer or even the entire network); this can usually be achieved by installing web-filtering software on the network. Training on how to detect cyber threats (e.g., phishing attempts in emails) and on what steps to take in case of malware and cyberattacks is critical. Many attacks happen through individual employee emails and similar sources.

5. **Protect financial assets from loss or theft.**

If the company interacts with the general public and employees have access to certain cash reserves, protocols should be in place to monitor the flow of money and require employees to balance cash at the end of their shifts. The company should also protect any reserves it has on-site by using a safe, and it should limit the funds it keeps on the premises to only the amount necessary to conduct daily business.

6. **Train employees on security practices and hold them accountable.**

Poor training often leads to security breaches, and thorough training conducted periodically will keep employees aware of and invested in the security of the business. This is especially true in regard to cybersecurity, whereby threats are transnational and organizations of any size are at risk.

EXAMPLES

4. What are OSHA's three levels of hazard mitigation?
    - **A)** train employees, test employees, protect employees
    - **B)** engineering controls, administrative controls, PPE
    - **C)** physical, health, psychosocial
    - **D)** policies, protection, restriction

5. Why should an organization develop written security policies and procedures?
   A) to outline policies and procedures to customers and clients
   B) to ensure policies and procedures are compliant with congressional regulations
   C) to clarify procedures to employees and show the organization is serious about security
   D) to keep policies and procedures on a "need to know" basis

Business Continuity

Organizations should be prepared for disasters like hurricanes, fires, terrorist attacks, pandemics, and other catastrophic events. HR practitioners are valuable partners in **business continuity** planning through the development of policies and procedures. Furthermore, they manage employee aspects of business continuity, including staffing plans, medical emergencies, PPE acquisition, allocation of resources, and other concerns. The planning and execution of business continuity processes are organized into four phases, as illustrated below.

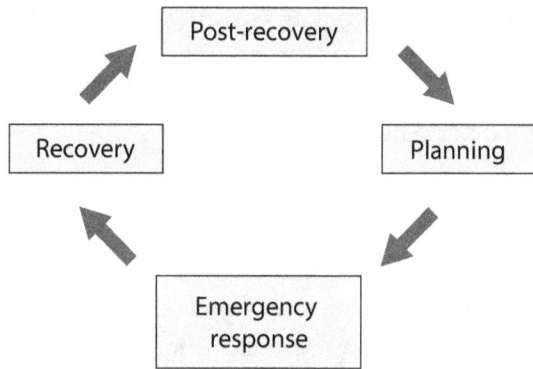

Figure 7.3. The Phases of Business Continuity

Planning Phase

During the planning phase, HR practitioners help the organization develop clear goals, procedures, and expectations that are then communicated to employees. Typically, these policies are included in the employee handbook, but they can also be contained in a stand-alone business continuity plan, and employees are trained and retrained on a periodic basis. The policies and procedures should outline important information the employees need to know, including:

- how the business will continue operations in the event of disaster
- the employee's role in maintaining contact with the employer
- how employees should handle certain hazards such as fire or power outages
- how the organization will notify employees of changes to business operations or safety procedures during a disaster

? **DID YOU KNOW?**

During the planning phase, HR professionals can use business analysis tools like the PESTLE analysis and the SWOT analysis. See chapter 1 for details on these tools.

Additionally, the business should develop a more detailed business continuity plan outlining asset recovery, employee mobilization, operations continuity, and compensation. The recovery plan should address all the logistics necessary to mitigate losses to the business, such as:

- Who is responsible for notifying authorities? How will first responders obtain access to the facilities?
- How will employees be evacuated? What will the company do to help employees find medical attention and safety if necessary?
- Where will employees work? Where will they stay? How will the company keep track of where employees are?
- How will employees be paid?
- What resources do they need to continue doing their jobs, such as mobile workstations or PPE, and how will the company provide these resources?
- How will the company's data, files, and information be protected to prevent disaster and recover from disaster? Are backup copies maintained remotely?

HR professionals play a key role in ensuring that the organization is ready to handle disasters and manage employees' whereabouts, safety, and business operations. Employees should understand their roles in the recovery process and should be trained periodically.

Recovery

During the **recovery** period, the organization must adapt to operating differently for a period of time. For example, employees may need to work remotely, certain services or production may be put on hold, or hours of operation may change. The HR department plays a critical role during this phase by working with managers to deploy and track staff and resources to keep the business operational. HR may notify employees of their roles, hours, and expectations of work during the recovery period. HR may also hire temporary staff if needed.

In addition, the HR department may respond to employees' immediate concerns and notify management of problems. HR can help fulfill employees' immediate needs by deploying emergency food, shelter, cash, or goods if the employee is required to be away from home and the normal worksite. Furthermore, if employees are ill or injured, HR can notify family members and keep them informed. Having these needs met will help able-bodied employees to keep the business running as smoothly as possible despite changes in conditions.

Post-Recovery

Once the recovery period has ended and the company is ready to resume operations, HR's role is to notify employees and help them transition back to normal operations. In the **post-recovery** period, if the surrounding area has been severely damaged, HR must respond to employees' needs for time off to find a new home, recover from injuries, or resolve personal and family matters.

During this period, it is important for the organization to remain flexible with employees and recognize their efforts to balance their personal and work responsibilities. Recognizing employees for their resilience and dedication to helping the organization succeed will keep morale higher. If employees feel that their needs are respected and that they are appreciated by the organization, they are more likely to remain loyal to the organization.

HR plays an important role during the planning and execution of business continuity procedures. If these processes are overlooked, the long-term success of the business and the well-being of employees may suffer. Involving HR, management, and employees in each step of the process and keeping communication open and clear will better position the organization to survive disaster and protect its employees and assets.

EXAMPLES

6. What tool might an HR practitioner use during the planning phase to determine what natural disasters could impact an organization?
    - **A)** monitoring KPIs
    - **B)** a PESTLE analysis
    - **C)** a SWOT analysis
    - **D)** Porter's Five Forces

7. How could HR determine what resources employees would need to continue working in case of an emergency and how to provide these resources?
    - **A)** the Hershey-Blanchard model
    - **B)** SMART goals
    - **C)** a SWOT analysis
    - **D)** French and Raven's Five Forms of Power

Privacy and Confidentiality

Privacy is the right to be unobserved. Managing an organization's safety and security can prompt privacy concerns. The organization needs to carefully monitor and protect its assets, but employees desire a degree of privacy in their daily activities. To manage risk, organizations may take measures like monitoring computer usage, conducting background checks of employees, and tracking people who enter and exit facilities.

In general, employees in the United States should have no broad expectation of privacy: The employer has a right to monitor and protect its assets. However, federal and state laws do protect the privacy of employees to an extent. When implementing certain measures, the organization must understand whether the activity is lawful. It must also weigh how effectively each practice achieves a specific business need.

Protected Information

Confidential information is private or secret information. While employees should not expect too much personal privacy in the workplace, there are certain forms of personal employee information that should be kept confidential or protected.

As a rule, only personally identifiable information such as a person's name or social security number is afforded special protection by data privacy laws. In some cases, a combination of information such as birth date, address, and gender can be used to identify an individual and is therefore considered **protected information**. Federal and state laws that govern the usage and sharing of personally identifiable information include:

- The **Health Insurance Portability and Accountability Act (HIPAA)** protects health-related information with covered entities such as insurance plans.
- The **Genetic Information Nondiscrimination Act (GINA)** protects and restricts the usage of employees' genetic information.
- The **Fair Credit Reporting Act (FCRA)** restricts the ways that consumer data, such as credit reports, may be used for employment purposes.

HELPFUL HINT
The Fair Credit Reporting Act requires employers to obtain written permission from applicants before conducting credit checks.

Many US states have their own laws concerning data security and notifications of breaches, and organizations should be aware of all data security laws in the states in which they operate. Additionally, companies have a legal responsibility to protect not only employee information but also that of job applicants, independent contractors, and customers. Companies that operate internationally should also be aware of the laws of each country in which they operate and implement security mechanisms to comply as legally required.

Even if there is no law that specifically requires the protection of certain data, it is still a best practice for the organization to ensure that all personal information, whether protected or not protected by law, is safe. Keeping active employees' data secure and discarding data that is no longer needed (as allowed by recordkeeping laws and regulations) can help mitigate the organization's risk. Employers can also protect data by disclosing it only to parties on a need-to-know basis, with the explicit authorization of the employee, or by virtue of a court order.

Data should be provided using the most secure means possible, like encrypted email, and there should be specific procedures in place to manage a data breach. Because HR professionals regularly work with personal data, it is important that they maintain confidentiality to the greatest extent possible and take careful measures not to compromise the security of data.

Workplace Monitoring and Searches

It is common for employers to **monitor** the computer, email, web, and phone usage of employees for quality control and security. They may also implement drug and alcohol testing to ensure the safety of employees and to prevent accidents or injuries.

Though some federal contractors and grantees may be required to provide a drug-free workplace, most private employers do not have any obligation to create a drug and alcohol policy or procedures. However, employers are legally required to provide a safe workplace, so it is important to assess which roles require employees to be free of drug or alcohol impairment. Such roles may include those employees who operate mechanical equipment or industrial trucks and vehicles, or who deal with critical data. When creating a drug and alcohol policy, it is important to consider laws such as the ADA, HIPAA, or the FLMA to ensure employees' rights are not infringed upon. Rather, build in interactive conversations, privacy, and other like issues to incorporate the needs of these many laws and regulations.

Beyond drug and alcohol testing, as a best practice and to comply with various privacy laws, the organization should notify employees (typically in a handbook) that they should have no expectation of privacy when on the premises or when using company resources and of the specific ways in which the company may monitor employees.

Companies should contact a qualified attorney to understand the legal limits of employee surveillance, drug testing, and personal searches. For example, companies may not put cameras in restrooms, but they may use cameras to monitor a cash register. Employers may also be limited in conduct of personal **searches** and may not force employees to submit to a search; however, they may rightfully terminate employees who refuse.

Clear policies that are applied consistently to all employees will help the organization set expectations and manage risk. If employees understand what is expected of them as well as the consequences for noncompliance, and if they understand that the rules are enforced universally, the organization can protect itself against claims of unfair treatment or discrimination while promoting a safe workplace.

EXAMPLES

8. The Fair Credit Reporting Act requires an employer to
    A) obtain written authorization from an applicant before conducting a credit check.
    B) use credit checks to verify an applicant's eligibility to work.
    C) conduct a credit check secretly.
    D) provide verbal notification that a credit check will be completed on a prospective employee.

9. Which of the following may an employer do in the workplace?
    A) force all employees to submit to personal searches
    B) place cameras anywhere in the workplace
    C) terminate any employee for drug or alcohol use
    D) monitor employees' company computer usage

Corporate Social Responsibility

HR plays a crucial role in corporate social responsibility. **Corporate social responsibility (CSR)** is how and to what level the organization focuses funds and capital toward improving one or more segments of society that are in need or are underrepresented by positively impacting their standard of living. Social responsibility is integrated into the business strategy through philanthropic endeavors like monetary or in-kind contributions, employee volunteerism, and community activities. Businesses can use social responsibility efforts not only to support specific causes but also to engage employees and create goodwill for the organization.

Organizations incorporating some level of social responsibility are generating long-term value for their shareholders because studies have shown that these types of programs can increase revenue and customer commitment.

Some larger organizations can have roles or departments that are specifically designed to carry out annual giving and participation throughout the year. This may include deciding, according to the strategic plan, who or which organizations receive funds and also what events should be attended. **Fundraising events** and galas are positive opportunities for an organization's profile. Large donors generally have the chance to receive high-level introductions, make speeches, and enjoy visibility through promotional items ("swag") made available to guests. Additionally, donations might come with tickets or seats to events that can be used in the entertainment of customers or employees, creating a win-win situation for both the giving and receiving organizations.

Community Inclusion

One way an organization can create community inclusion is through philanthropic efforts. **Philanthropy** can include the donation of monies or employees' time and talents.

Many organizations practice charitable giving. **Charitable giving** may be as simple as the company itself donating funds to one or more specific nonprofit organizations. It may also be conducted through providing mechanisms for the employees to donate. Payroll deductions or matching contributions are some of the ways businesses can encourage and support personnel donating their own funds.

One way an organization may enact corporate social responsibility is through a **volunteer program** or policy. In these programs, employees are encouraged to volunteer their time to nonprofit organizations, especially through incentives like paid time off for volunteer time or bonuses tied to volunteering. HR can work with organizational leaders to create a volunteerism policy and promote it throughout the organization. Typically, these policies include information around which organization(s) or what types of services the employee can provide to receive their corporate-sponsored benefits by volunteering.

Additionally, organizations might even organize volunteer events or days of service where groups of individuals have the opportunity to work together on a project. This not only supports the selected organization; it also creates a team-building opportunity for the company.

Another type of volunteering an organization might encourage is for employees to join and participate on **boards of directors** for specific or defined organizations. This is done not only to support these nonprofit organizations but also to help grow employees as they are exposed to the strategic decision-making and financial planning as board members. Additionally, participation on boards can spread goodwill for the organization as name recognition is expanded.

Corporate Citizenship

All of these philanthropic efforts support a business's corporate citizenship. **Corporate citizenship** refers to an organization's responsibility to creating a higher standard of living or improving the quality of life of its neighboring communities, or other areas throughout the globe.

Corporate responsibility not only includes charitable giving; it also extends to the moral and ethical treatment of an organization's suppliers, employees, distributors, and customers. That is, in addition to simply donating money, the corporation integrates its designated causes and annual agendas into their overall strategy.

EXAMPLE

10. Which of the following is an example of corporate social responsibility?
    A) an employee donates to a political campaign and lists their place of work on the form
    B) the company sponsors a group of employees volunteering at a beach clean-up
    C) a company pays taxes owed to the state and federal governments
    D) an employee volunteers at their church in their spare time on the weekend

Answer Key

1. **A)** The definition of risk is the probability that a specific outcome (or harm) will occur.

2. **D)** Risk management focuses on protecting the business and employees from external factors.

3. **D)** Regulations are specific directives with the same force of law enacted by federal agencies in order to execute acts of Congress.

4. **B)** OSHA's three levels of hazard mitigation or control are engineering controls, administrative controls, and personal protective equipment (PPE).

5. **C)** Documented security policies and procedures accessible to employees show the organization's commitment to security and clarify procedures to management. Written policies facilitate the enforcement of security concerns on a day-to-day basis.

6. **B)** A PESTLE analysis shows how external factors (political, economic, social, technological, legal, and environmental) may impact an organization. For instance, environmental factors like hurricanes or wildfires might impact an organization's day-to-day operations. A PESTLE analysis would reveal those specific factors.

7. **C)** A SWOT analysis examines internal strengths and weaknesses and external opportunities and threats. In the planning phase, HR could outline resources, like existing facilities, workstations, budgets, and technical skills, under "strengths." Then, HR could determine what is still needed for employees who might need to work from home in case of a pandemic or natural disaster. For example, the organization might have a shortage of laptop computers with cameras, a shortage of remote workstations, or no budget for remote working programs that require a monthly subscription. Those could go under "weaknesses," and HR could plan accordingly to resolve those shortcomings.

8. **A)** According to the Fair Credit Reporting Act, employers must have written authorization from an applicant before conducting a credit check.

9. **D)** Employers may monitor employees' use of company computers.

10. **B)** A group of employees participating in a volunteer clean-up event is a great example of corporate social responsibility through volunteerism and is also a good way to build teamwork and camaraderie.

8 SHRM Practice Test

Knowledge-Based Questions

Directions: Read the question, then choose the best answer.

1. Your organization is considering a merger. As the human resources manager, what activities should you be conducting before the deal has closed and before integration has started?
   A) addressing key HR processes
   B) recognizing cultural differences
   C) identifying conflicts
   D) optimizing the workforce

2. What is the perceived fairness of a process called?
   A) distributive justice
   B) equality
   C) procedural justice
   D) external equity

3. When designing training for the adult learner, what design ideas should be considered?
   A) Adult learners need to know why they are learning something.
   B) Adult learners have more time to focus on training because they are done with formal schooling.
   C) Adult learners do not like to spend time practicing, so reinforcement is not needed.
   D) Adult learners respond better to lectures than to hands-on training.

4. Which of the following evaluates the relative value of one job against all jobs in a single organization?
   A) compensable factors
   B) job analysis
   C) compensation surveys
   D) internal consistency

5. There are many laws that protect workers' rights when it comes to pay and pay discrimination. Which of the following laws is NOT designed to provide this type of protection?
   A) Equal Pay Act of 1963
   B) Title VII of the Civil Rights Act of 1964
   C) Age Discrimination in Employment Act of 1967
   D) Consolidated Omnibus Budget Reconciliation Act of 1984

6. As the human resources manager, which of the following question types would you encourage your hiring manager to use in an interview?
   A) yes and no questions
   B) leading questions
   C) situational questions
   D) personal questions

137

7. Which of the following refers to a survey conducted when an employee leaves an organization?
   A) termination questionnaire
   B) attitude survey
   C) exit interview
   D) retention evaluation

8. Sally and Bill are both managers at a local manufacturer. They have been dating for about a year and appear to be getting along quite well. However, their supervisor has noted that they have been spending a significant time away from their desks at the same time, and this is impacting the organization's overall performance. What might this be an example of?
   A) hostile work environment
   B) nepotism
   C) inadvisable dating in the workplace
   D) quid pro quo

9. A company's guideline indicates that employees must be at least 5'7" and 200 pounds to drive a piece of equipment. This guideline has been in place for several years for the safety of the crew. However, there are no official guidelines that this type of restriction is needed. For which reason might this situation potentially be illegal?
   A) disparate treatment
   B) OSHA regulation deviation
   C) disparate impact
   D) restrictive covenant

10. The human resources manager has created a document listing all of the requisite education, skills, and abilities needed to perform a specific role. What is this document called?
    A) job description
    B) job specification
    C) job analysis
    D) job requisition

11. Barbara and her supervisor both enjoy football. They get together on Sundays to watch the games with their families and often talk football in the office. When it is time to complete Barbara's performance review, her boss is unduly influenced by their shared love of football. This is an example of which type of rater error?
    A) horns effect
    B) recency effect
    C) central tendency
    D) similar-to-me effect

12. One measurement you can use to evaluate the recruitment process is the comparison between the number of applicants per stage of hire and the number that moves onto the next stage of hire. What is this metric called?
    A) yield ratio
    B) recruitment costs
    C) selection ratio
    D) acceptance rate

13. As part of the hiring process, a scenario is set up in which candidates must make decisions about a customer concern. This is an example of which type of testing?
    A) physical abilities test
    B) cognitive abilities test
    C) situational judgment test
    D) work sample test

14. Carl supervises a team of accountants in Michigan. He is hot-tempered, screaming at individuals and blowing up over the smallest errors. He micromanages and rides employees when they are given assignments. When he is in a particularly bad mood, he likes to choose one person to focus his negative attention on. The team is always on edge because they do not know when they might be the focus of Carl's rants. What is this an example of?
    A) bullying
    B) illegal harassment
    C) wage and hour violation
    D) nepotism

15. When settling a labor contract, if the two parties cannot come to an agreement, they may use a third party to make a final decision. What is this process called?
    A) conciliation
    B) arbitration
    C) pacification
    D) ratification

16. The hiring manager is sharing her list of questions with you so that you can note which ones might be discriminatory. Which of the following questions is most likely NOT discriminatory?
    A) Did you graduate from high school?
    B) Where did you go to high school?
    C) What year did you graduate?
    D) What is the origin of your last name?

17. An employer can take steps to prevent unionization. However, there are specific actions that are considered illegal under the NLRB and other requirements. Which of the following would be considered LEGAL action?
    A) explaining to employees that the plant will close down if the union is voted in
    B) telling employees the disadvantages of having a union
    C) surveying employees to determine how they will vote
    D) asking for information or attending union organization meetings

18. When creating an offer of employment, which of the following is inappropriate to include?
    A) job details
    B) pay-related items
    C) employee benefits summary
    D) permanent or temporary status

19. Your payroll clerk has been performing well. She currently enters time and attendance and is interested in taking on more responsibilities, so you add verification and payroll run to her duties. This is an example of what type of job redesign?
    A) job enlargement
    B) job enrichment
    C) job rotation
    D) task significance

20. An organization has recently made productivity improvements by eliminating layers, changing reporting relationships, and downsizing certain departments. What is this type of initiative called?
    A) redesigning work
    B) aligning human capital activities
    C) organizational restructuring
    D) waste elimination coordination

21. During a strategic planning session, the human resources manager obtained data about internal metrics such as head count, cost of recruitment, and yield ratio, along with external information including market pay and unemployment rates. What is this process called?
    A) wage analysis
    B) environmental scanning
    C) human resources planning
    D) PESTLE analysis

22. An organization that is reducing the number of hours employees are working, initiating a hiring freeze, and offering a voluntary separation program may be implementing strategy to manage which of the following?
    A) a talent shortage
    B) redesigning work
    C) a merger or acquisition
    D) a talent surplus

23. An employee who is paid a fixed amount but also qualifies for overtime pay falls into which classification?
    A) salaried
    B) hourly
    C) salaried nonexempt
    D) exempt

24. Which of the following is the BEST example of a BFOQ?
    A) a manufacturing facility that requires an individual to be able to lift their 30-pound products
    B) a marketing agency that requires a personality test as part of the interview process
    C) a construction company that requires fall protection use
    D) an Italian restaurant that hires only female servers

25. Title VII of the Civil Rights Act applies to all organizations EXCEPT
    A) private employers of 10 or fewer employees.
    B) state and local governments.
    C) private employment agencies.
    D) educational institutions.

26. Flexibility in staffing levels and access to subject-matter experts are advantages of using
    A) a professional employer organization.
    B) a recruitment agency.
    C) independent contractors.
    D) employee referrals.

27. A firm completes a study of its workforce and discovers that racial and ethical underrepresentation exist throughout its internal population. Which of the following steps might the firm take to correct this issue?
    A) ask employees to mention open roles on their social media sites
    B) institute an employee referral program
    C) initiate an anonymous application procedure
    D) employ personality testing to assess cultural fit in an unbiased manner

28. An organization that just established a flexible-hours policy, increased the number of jobs with a telecommuting option, and scheduled compressed workweeks may be trying to do what?
    A) help employees balance work-life issues
    B) find cost reduction in wages
    C) comply with OSHA regulations
    D) manage pay compression

29. Jane and Deb have been dating for a few months, and Jane is Deb's boss. Deb has told a friend she wishes she could break it off with Jane. However, raises are scheduled for next month, and Jane has implied that Deb will get a large bonus if she remains Jane's girlfriend. What might this be an example of?
    A) hostile work environment
    B) nepotism
    C) inadvisable dating in the workplace
    D) quid pro quo

30. Under the Americans with Disabilities Act (ADA) an employer cannot discriminate against an individual who is "regarded as disabled." Which of the following is an example of "regarded as disabled"?
    A) an individual who has been disfigured from a severe burn but has no restrictions
    B) an individual who uses a wheelchair but is able to perform the essential functions of the job
    C) an individual who has a spouse with a significant disability that limits their essential life functions
    D) an individual who is recovering from an addiction but is able to be present at work

31. Cost of testing, background checks, relocation, and signing bonus are examples of expenses that could be included when computing which of the following?
    A) yield ratio
    B) cost of recruiting
    C) acceptance costs
    D) selection ratio

32. Which of the following cases first recognized a hostile work environment as sexual discrimination under Title VII?
    A) *Burlington Industries Inc. vs. Ellerth*
    B) *Green vs. Brennan*
    C) *Meritor Savings Bank vs. Vinson*
    D) *Griggs vs. Duke Power Co.*

33. When determining the essential functions of a job, all of the following are acceptable to use in the analysis EXCEPT
    A) the amount of time spent performing the function.
    B) the number of employees available who can perform the function.
    C) the highly specialized nature of the function.
    D) the fact that the function is included in the job description.

34. During a layoff, a firm contracts with an organization to support terminated employees in their job search. What is this an example of?
    A) job elimination
    B) downsizing assistance

Elissa Simon | SHRM CP EXAM PREP

C) outplacement services
D) temporary services

35. Though Juan was born and raised in Michigan, he is of Mexican descent. His coworkers have nicknamed him "Speedy Gonzales" because, they say, he is the fastest person on the line. They also make jokes about him being an alien and constantly ask him "how" he got to the States. On Cinco de Mayo they placed Mexican flags all over his locker. In the break room they constantly make comments about his food, asking why he did not bring tacos or burritos for lunch. Though Juan thought this treatment was funny at first, now he dreads coming to work and his productivity is starting to fall due to stress. What is this situation an example of?
    A) quid pro quo
    B) diversification breakdown
    C) hostile work environment
    D) affirmative action

36. A human resources department is assessing its performance compared to other divisions and organizations. What is this is an example of?
    A) benchmarking
    B) balanced scorecard
    C) human resources audit
    D) human resources metrics

37. An employee born in 1968 is part of which generation?
    A) Baby Boomers
    B) Millennials
    C) Silent Generation
    D) Generation X

38. Which of the following BEST describes the psychological contract?
    A) elements included in the offer letter upon entry into a workplace
    B) unwritten expectations between an employer and employee
    C) a supported bias to sustain a specific culture
    D) an agreement with an employee assistance program to offer services

39. Which of the following refers to the failure to report to work per the job schedule or to stay at work through a shift?
    A) turnover
    B) tardiness
    C) job dissatisfaction
    D) absenteeism

40. The Pregnancy Discrimination Act requires employers of fifteen or more people to do which of the following?
    A) offer family and medical leave
    B) treat maternity as any other leave
    C) offer six weeks of paid leave
    D) designate a space for nursing mothers

41. An organization may use separation costs, replacement costs, and training costs to measure which of the following?
    A) turnover costs
    B) recruitment costs
    C) absenteeism costs
    D) job satisfaction

42. Title VII of the Civil Rights Act covers private employers with more than ____ employees.
    A) 1
    B) 15
    C) 50
    D) 100

43. Which of the following would be considered a reasonable accommodation under the Americans with Disabilities Act (ADA)?
    A) purchase of a wheelchair
    B) screen-reading software
    C) monitoring employee medications
    D) providing hearing aids

44. An organization identifies a deficiency within its workforce regarding diversity and implements an initiative to recruit persons of a specific protected class. This is an example of which of the following?
    A) equal employment
    B) disparate treatment
    C) affirmative action
    D) accommodation

45. A supervisor states that he does not want to hire anyone with an Italian background. This is an example of discrimination based on which protected class?
   A) race
   B) religion
   C) national origin
   D) color

46. Which of the following requires private employers to provide reasonable accommodations for individuals with disabilities?
   A) Vocational Rehabilitation Act
   B) Executive Order 11478
   C) Civil Rights Act
   D) ADA

47. Anthony works in a high-stress job that requires a significant amount of creativity. His organization has offered to give him three months off with pay so he can travel and rejuvenate. What is this type of benefit called?
   A) PTO
   B) vacation
   C) sabbatical
   D) leave of absence

48. Craig was a good performer all year, but in the last few weeks he has missed a significant amount of time to tend to his aging mother. His supervisor gave him a poor rating because of this change in behavior. This is an example of which type of rater error?
   A) varying standards
   B) sampling error
   C) recency effect
   D) central tendency

49. What is the set of shared values and beliefs that govern an organization?
   A) psychological contract
   B) organizational culture
   C) vision statement
   D) organizational convention

50. An employee is fired two days after filing a discrimination complaint with his manager. It appears that which of the following may have occurred?
   A) disparate treatment
   B) disparate impact
   C) harassment
   D) retaliation

51. The term turnover describes the number of and reasons for employees leaving an organization. Which of the following is NOT a type of turnover?
   A) involuntary
   B) voluntary
   C) controlled
   D) no fault

52. During an interview, the hiring manager realizes that he graduated from the same high school as the candidate. He asks what year the candidate graduated to see if they share any common friends. What type of discrimination could occur as a result of this question?
   A) familial status
   B) citizenship
   C) age
   D) disability

53. You are participating in an interview scheduled during the week before Easter. The hiring manager is making small talk with the candidate and asks what Easter traditions their family celebrates. What type of discrimination could occur as a result of this question?
   A) gender
   B) age
   C) religion
   D) disability

54. During union negotiations, the two sides have failed to reach an agreement. In order to put pressure on the company, the employees refuse to work. Additionally, they have begun to picket and carry signs. What is this demonstration called?
   A) unfair labor practice strike
   B) wildcat strike
   C) jurisdictional strike
   D) economic strike

55. When deciding on a relocation area, it is important to look at the pool of candidates in that area. What is this local candidate supply called?
- A) the labor market
- B) the applicant pool
- C) the unemployment rate
- D) the outsourcing market

56. Which of the following types of organizations do NOT have to complete the EEO-1 annual reporting form?
- A) private employers with 100 or more employees
- B) state and local governments
- C) federal contractors with fifty or more employees and $50,000 or more in contracts
- D) financial institutions with fifty or more employees and that hold government funds or bonds

57. One method of job redesign is to expand the scope of the job by adding additional tasks or responsibilities. What is this process called?
- A) job enlargement
- B) job enrichment
- C) job rotation
- D) task significance

58. Employees were complaining about boredom and muscle fatigue, so management developed a schedule to move them from one work center to the next throughout the day. What is this method of job redesign called?
- A) job enlargement
- B) job enrichment
- C) job rotation
- D) task significance

59. Which of the following requires federal contractors and subcontractors to implement affirmative action to eliminate discrimination?
- A) Title VII
- B) Executive Order 11246 as amended by 11375
- C) Congressional Accountability Act
- D) Executive Order 11478

60. An employer felt extreme pressure to hire since production was suffering. A person who stopped by to inquire about employment was hired on the spot. No references or background checks were done. Later, this person was violent in the workplace and hurt another employee. It was discovered that the new hire had a criminal record including felony assault. This is an example of
- A) halo error.
- B) nondirective interview process.
- C) negligent hiring.
- D) poor advertising.

61. Which of the following would be a job specification for an accounting role?
- A) laptop computer
- B) bachelor's degree in accounting
- C) quarter-end reporting
- D) supervises three individuals

62. The HR manager would like to clarify job expectations and key performance indicators. What tool should the manager create?
- A) job specifications
- B) job analysis
- C) performance standards
- D) work sample

63. When performing a job analysis, what does the initial stage of the planning process include?
- A) review and compile data
- B) review existing job documents
- C) identify the objective of the job analysis
- D) update the job descriptions

64. Which of the following is an advantage of using a questionnaire during a job analysis?
- A) It is widely used and accepted.
- B) Information on a large number of jobs can be collected.
- C) It allows for clarification and verification.
- D) It can measure literacy at the same time.

CONTINUE

65. Which term refers to the section of a job description that indicates an employee is hired at at-will status and allows an employer to change employee duties?
    A) identification
    B) summary
    C) functions and duties
    D) disclaimer

66. When creating a job description, the job specification section should include language clarifying which of the following?
    A) the essential functions of the job
    B) the required knowledge, skills, and abilities
    C) the tasks and duties to be performed
    D) a summary of the scope of the role

67. Which of the following agencies ensures that federal contractors use nondiscriminatory practices?
    A) EEOC
    B) OFCCP
    C) NLRB
    D) DOL

68. If the director of HR asks how many candidates are in the applicant pool, which number would you give her?
    A) the total number of individuals who are available for selection
    B) the total number of individuals who have been evaluated for selection
    C) the total number of individuals selected for a final interview
    D) the total number of hires versus applicants

69. What is an organization that supplies its own workforce to an employer?
    A) an employment-leasing organization
    B) a professional employer organization
    C) a recruitment agency
    D) an outsourcing firm

70. An employer can legally justify difference in pay under the Equal Pay Act if which of the following is true?
    A) The difference is attributed to seniority and market rates.
    B) The difference is attributed to quality of work and natural progression of previous wages.
    C) The difference is attributed to performance and seniority.
    D) The difference is attributed to internal equity within a specific department.

71. Interns sometimes complain that they are not fully utilized during their time at an organization. What step could an organization take to offer a successful internship experience?
    A) pay reasonably but below full-time employees
    B) take advantage of the help and finish off mundane projects
    C) plan ahead of time and decide what the company really needs
    D) do not bore intern with new-hire paperwork

72. When creating an employment application, it is advised to include all of the following EXCEPT
    A) an at-will employment statement.
    B) notification of employment testing.
    C) request for permission to contact references.
    D) space for an employee's social security number.

73. Which of the following should NOT be included in the "personal information" section of an employment application?
    A) name
    B) address
    C) date of birth
    D) phone number

74. In testing, validity refers to what?
    A) consistency of the test between applicants
    B) the extent to which the test measures what it intends to measure
    C) the measurement of personality characteristics
    D) the fit of the right person to the culture of the organization

75. What process is designed to measure individual performance, coach and develop employees, and reward and recognize performance?
    A) performance management
    B) pay-for-performance
    C) predictive validity
    D) psychological contract

76. Kendra has taken a role overseas with her organization. This is a two-year role after which she will return to her home country. While working abroad, what is Kendra considered?
    A) an expatriate
    B) reassigned
    C) repatriated
    D) on sabbatical

77. A former employee has submitted a claim with the EEOC and received a "right to sue" letter. What does this mean?
    A) The EEOC acknowledges their complaint submission.
    B) The complaint will be moving into mediation.
    C) The complainant has a right to sue in federal court.
    D) The EEOC has determined it has jurisdiction.

78. An employee who must be paid overtime for working over 40 hours in a week is considered what?
    A) hourly
    B) nonexempt
    C) exempt
    D) salaried

79. You designed a physical abilities test internally. The supervisor administered the test before you had a chance to validate it. Which act could you unintentionally be violating?
    A) FLSA
    B) ADA
    C) OSHA
    D) Immigration Reform and Control Act

80. Which of the following terms refers to the process new employees undergo to learn about the organization, their role, and their coworkers?
    A) onboarding
    B) job shadowing
    C) coaching
    D) on-the-job training

Situational Judgment Questions

Directions: These questions are based on realistic workplace scenarios. Each scenario is followed by two or three questions. Read the short description of the scenario. Then answer the questions based on how you would respond in a workplace setting.

You are the human resources manager for a small manufacturing organization that is located in an area with a diverse population but does not have a lot of internal diversity. Your company has set the goal of increasing diversity within the organization. One of your managers is interviewing candidates for an open role.

81. What could you do to improve the recruitment process?
    A) create a structured questionnaire based on the job specifications for the manager to follow
    B) offer a signing bonus to encourage applicants
    C) create an employee referral program
    D) have a second interview in an informal setting to measure cultural fit

82. Another step you might take is offering diversity and inclusion training to your management or hiring team. Which of the following training topics would be MOST relevant to this situation?
    A) an open conversation around gender discrimination and harassment avoidance
    B) an overview of the application system and how it can track the interviewing process
    C) a review of diversity and inclusion laws like Title VII and how they apply to the interview process
    D) an analysis of the accommodation policy to ensure the ADA and ADEA are not being violated

An organization with forty employees is having trouble meeting its budget and controlling cost. One area of the budget that must be assessed is benefits costs. The organization needs to assess if any changes could be made to help control costs and get the business back into the black.

83. You have been asked to compute the health care benefits cost per employee. This is an example of measuring
    A) total compensation.
    B) benefits effectiveness.
    C) benefits responsiveness.
    D) benefits cash balance.

84. When assessing the benefits program, which of the following is a discretionary benefit that the organization can choose NOT to offer?
    A) workers' compensation
    B) health insurance
    C) unemployment insurance
    D) social security

You are the human resources manager for an organization that grew from forty-five employees last year to fifty-five employees this year. You must now administer the Family and Medical Leave Act because organizations of this size are required to comply with the FMLA.

85. A new employee has requested FMLA leave because of their child's serious health condition. You check the employee records and see they have been employed for eight months. You explain that this employee is
    A) eligible for leave because it is for an immediate family member's serious health condition.
    B) eligible for leave because they have worked more than 1,250 hours in the year.
    C) not eligible for leave because they have been employed for fewer than twelve months.
    D) not eligible for leave because it is not for their own serious health condition.

86. Another employee comes to request a leave. This person works full-time and has been with the organization for six years. The employee wishes to take FMLA leave to visit a close cousin who is dying of cancer. You explain to the employee that they are
    A) eligible for leave because they have worked more than 1,250 hours in the year.
    B) eligible for leave because they have been employed for more than twelve months.
    C) not eligible for leave because it is not to care for a spouse, child, or parent with a serious health condition.
    D) not eligible for leave because the cousin is not a minor or over the age of sixty-five.

An employee has a heart attack while at work covering a holiday shift. His coworkers call 911, and he goes to the hospital. Fortunately, the heart attack was mild, and the employee will recover. The employee works in production for a 100-person organization that makes parts for the auto industry.

87. How would you determine if this situation should be covered under workers' compensation?
    A) Because it happened at work, it is automatically a workers' compensation claim.
    B) Because the medical event was a heart attack, it cannot be considered a workers' compensation claim.
    C) An analysis must be conducted of the medical event and the duties the employee was asked to complete.
    D) The employee was working a holiday shift, so it cannot be considered a workers' compensation claim.

88. Several laws and regulations apply in a situation like this. What laws need to be considered?
    A) FMLA, ADA, and OSHA
    B) FMLA and Title VII
    C) unemployment insurance and ADA
    D) OSHA, ACA, and ADEA

Your organization has just grown to over thirty-five employees. Currently your organization does not have a human resources function but is considering adding support. As the office manager, you must conduct an analysis on the possibility of adding human resources, and you are looking for specific recommendations.

89. Your research indicates that one large contribution human resources can make is during the _____ process, by providing analysis and design of work, HR planning, and HR analytics.
    A) hiring
    B) performance feedback
    C) communication
    D) strategic management

90. After review, you recommend that the organization contract with a local provider to perform specific human resources services. What is this called?
    A) shared services
    B) self-services
    C) outsourcing
    D) temporary services

Ben works in the human resources department and has been asked to complete a job analysis of the accounting department. This department is composed of five individuals who all perform unique roles.

91. While analyzing the cost accounting role, Ben identifies certain skills and abilities, such as a mastery of spreadsheets and a full understanding of the balance sheet, needed to perform this job. What are these identified skills and abilities considered?
    A) job descriptions
    B) job requirements
    C) performance standards
    D) job specifications

92. Ben is using the job analysis data to create a job description. When looking at the senior accountant role, he identified that this job creates month-end reports and reconciles the bank balances. In which section of the job description would he include these two items?
    A) identification
    B) general summary
    C) essential functions and duties
    D) job specifications

Carla is seventy-five years old and still works full-time. She is a nurse with a local mental health agency working to dispense medications to patients. She has been with the agency for almost forty years. She has a good relationship with her supervisor and can be relied upon to be at work every day. She has given no indication of retiring and appears to be enjoying her job.

93. Over the last twelve to eighteen months, Carla has made an increasing number of mistakes. She seems easily confused and is double-entering information. What is the first step her supervisor should take?
    A) explain to Carla it is time to retire and offer to buy her a parting gift
    B) demote Carla to a role that is less complicated
    C) sit down with Carla to review the mistakes and together develop goals to improve her performance
    D) do nothing since Carla knows her role and is most likely close to retirement anyway

94. The owner of the company indicates he would like Carla to resign since she is older; he says, "it is time for some young blood." Carla's supervisor does not agree because the mistakes have occurred only in the last few months, and Carla has been a good performer. If the owner proceeded with demanding Carla retire, what law might he be violating?

    A) Title VII
    B) ADEA
    C) ADA
    D) ACA

Vicky is the new training coordinator for an automotive supply company. She has many years of experience and has been hired to develop programs to improve productivity and quality. The organization has been struggling with the number of returns, which is impacting financial performance.

95. What is the first step Vicky should take to develop a training program for manufacturing?

    A) develop learning objectives
    B) develop training materials
    C) perform a training needs assessment
    D) implement the training

96. When developing the learning objectives, which items should Vicky consider?

    A) the participants' learning styles, content, materials, and learning theories
    B) weighted biodata assessed from preemployment screening
    C) an evaluation and feedback to adjust the program as needed
    D) the schedule and location for the training

Greg, an HR manager, has been asked to fly to a sister company to investigate a sexual harassment complaint. Though he has visited the location before, he is not acquainted with the accused or the accuser. He has been asked to conduct the investigation as a neutral third-party to ensure it is done in a fair manner.

97. When Greg arrives onsite and begins the investigation, what is a good first step?

    A) have a company-wide meeting to explain his visit and state that he will meet with several individuals
    B) meet with the accused first so that he has a good idea of the accused's side of the story
    C) meet with the witnesses first since their memory and testimony may change over time
    D) meet with the accuser first to hear the accuser's side of the story and understand the complaint

98. At the end of the investigation, while typing up the details, Greg notes that there were never any requests for sexual favors. Rather, the evidence shows that repeated offensive jokes were told, that crude language was often used, and that pornographic pictures were posted near the accuser's locker. This evidence points toward which type of sexual harassment?

    A) quid pro quo
    B) disparate impact
    C) hostile work environment
    D) disparate treatment

A local travel agent services clients from all around the United States. Therefore, the company must cover several different time zones, so employees need to be in the office from 7:00 a.m. to 9:00 p.m. Two shifts cover this period: one starts at 7:00 a.m. and ends at 4:00 p.m., and the other starts at noon and ends at 9:00 p.m.

99. Employees have complained that there are very few calls before 10:00 a.m. and after 7:00 p.m. Management analyzes call demand and considers employee complaints. They propose a schedule in which a specific level of coverage during "core hours" is required, but otherwise employees may vary their start and stop times. What is this an example of?

    A) compressed workweek
    B) flex time
    C) telecommuting
    D) controlled staffing

100. During the summer months, the organization allows the employees to work four ten-hour days. One group works Monday through Thursday, and the other works Tuesday through Friday. What is this an example of?

A) compressed workweek
B) flex time
C) telecommuting
D) controlled staffing

Trisha works in the human resources department and has been asked to complete a job analysis of the manufacturing department. This department is composed of forty machine operators who work on a variety of different equipment making automotive parts.

101. What is the first step Trisha should take in performing a job analysis?

A) select a method
B) review data collected
C) identify the job(s) to be analyzed
D) collect relevant data

102. Trisha decides to perform the job analysis by going out to the factory floor to watch the different operations. What is this type of analysis called?

A) interviewing
B) questionnaire
C) observation
D) functional job analysis

You have recently been hired as the HR manager for an organization. When you first arrive, you find that an employee had asked for a headset to wear when working with customers because she was struggling with hearing loss due to a childhood injury. You have been told that this request was denied because the employee was a poor performer.

103. Which law are you concerned might have been broken in this situation?

A) the Pregnancy Discrimination Act
B) Executive Order 11246
C) the ADA
D) Title VII

104. Looking into the situation, you find that the requested headset would have cost less than $100. What is this an example of?

A) equipment requisition
B) reasonable accommodation
C) undue hardship
D) harassment

Roberto is a human resources director working with a hiring manager on an open role in the manager's department. Roberto has already completed a job analysis and a job description for the role. The next steps to fill the role focus on advertisement and gathering candidates.

105. Due to the nature of the job, Roberto decides that the best options for attracting the right candidates are to advertise the role on social media and on a local radio station. Roberto has decided on the

A) recruiting method.
B) applicant pool.
C) labor market.
D) recruiting message.

106. Roberto develops a description of the company and the role, including explaining why someone might be interested in applying. Roberto has created the

A) recruiting method.
B) applicant pool.
C) labor market.
D) recruiting message.

CONTINUE

Tonya works as the office manager for a smaller company. She has many responsibilities that are part of a typical human resources function, including recruitment and selection. She has recently been asked to hire a new person in customer service.

107. Tonya uses the company's HRIS system, posts the opening on the intranet, and creates an employee referral program. All of these efforts are considered
    A) direct sources.
    B) automatic sources.
    C) internal sources.
    D) advertising sources.

108. Tonya eventually found and hired a candidate through a private third party. The company paid the third party an amount equal to 30 percent of the candidate's first-year salary. What is this type of organization called?
    A) labor union
    B) temporary agency
    C) job fair
    D) employment agency

Brimmer is a 150-person organization that produces parts for the aerospace industry. Fred is the HR manager. He must ensure Brimmer is in compliance with HR laws and regulations, including any reporting requirements.

109. Since Brimmer has more than 100 employees, the company is required to complete which of the following?
    A) OSHA 300A
    B) EEO-1
    C) an affirmative action plan
    D) application disclaimer notice

110. Fred meets with the sales department and learns that the company is not a federal contractor because it does not sell parts directly to the government. What else might require Brimmer to create an affirmative action plan?
    A) Brimmer is a subcontractor that supplies over $10,000 in parts to a federal contractor.
    B) Brimmer contracts with a foreign government and supplies it with more than $10,000 in parts.
    C) Brimmer employs US military veterans.
    D) Brimmer buys $10,000 of product from a federal contractor.

Shannon works for a human resources outsourcing company and has been asked to perform an audit on an organization's processes. This organization has approximately twenty employees and is only a few years old. Though the managers know a lot about making their product, they do not know the laws surrounding human resources practices. When Shannon comes in, they have several questions about the hiring process.

111. When Shannon reviewed the hiring application, she saw many illegal questions asking about protected information. Which of the following is LEGAL to ask about on an employment application?
    A) marital status of the applicant
    B) number and ages of dependents
    C) date of high school graduation
    D) whether the applicant is over eighteen

112. When verifying eligibility to work in the United States, which document is NOT acceptable to use?
    A) driver's license
    B) US passport
    C) foreign birth certificate
    D) social security card

Chris works for a metal stamping company. Work conditions are very hot, especially in the summer, and loud during most of the shift. Employees are required to wear significant personal protective equipment and to manually move heavy parts. The company has a good reputation for treating their employees well, but the work is difficult.

113. When Chris is interviewing candidates, he takes extra time to explain how difficult the job is, that the personal protective equipment can be uncomfortable, and that the plant is hot in the summer. He also takes time to walk the candidates through the shop so they can see the working conditions. What process is Chris is following?
    A) failure to project
    B) informed interviewing
    C) realistic job preview
    D) job ability discussion

114. Due to the nature of the job, Chris wants to ensure that any new hire is physically able to perform the tasks. What steps should Chris take to include a physical ability test?
    A) due to cost, test only those individuals who appear unlikely to be able to perform the role
    B) send the top three candidates to the occupational physician, who will decide who should be hired
    C) offer the job to the top candidate, but make it contingent on passing a physical by the occupational physician
    D) before interviewing a candidate, require each person to submit a fit-for-duty slip from their personal physician

The company has been interviewing candidates for an open role. You had set up a list of questions for the hiring manager but recently found out that she has been deviating from these questions. You ask to discuss the matter with her. You learn that some of the questions she has been asking may violate specific laws.

115. The hiring manager has a passion for safety. During your meeting, you learn that she has been asking candidates if they have ever filed for workers' compensation and, if so, what was the injury. Which law does this question likely violate?
    A) Title VII
    B) ADEA
    C) OSHA
    D) ADA

116. The company runs a shift on Sundays. During your meeting, you learn that the hiring manager has been concerned about candidates being available to work Sundays, so she has been asking where they go to church and how often they attend. Which law does this question likely violate?
    A) Title VII
    B) ADEA
    C) OSHA
    D) ADA

Dan is the human resources manager at a hospital. The nurses have started a campaign to bring in the union to represent them. Dan knows there are many things that he and the managers should avoid saying or doing so they will not violate the NLRA. It is Dan's role to educate the other managers at the hospital.

117. Dan teaches the managers the TIPS rule. This is an easy acronym to help them remember what they can and cannot say. What does TIPS stand for?
    A) training independence in personnel situations
    B) threats, interrogation, promises, and surveillance
    C) timing, induction, presence, and sympathy
    D) treat individuals with preferred security

118. Dan has learned that one of the managers has violated the TIPS rule. Which of the following would violate TIPS?
    A) telling the nurses that the manager and the hospital are opposed to unionization
    B) reminding nurses that they do not have to speak to union organizers or let organizers visit them at home
    C) transferring or punishing nurses with less desirable work
    D) explaining to nurses that the union cannot guarantee results

You have just been promoted to vice president of human resources. In this role you are part of the executive committee and responsible for strategic planning. At your company, strategic planning means supporting the executive committee and creating a strategic vision for the human resources function.

119. To support your department and organization, you create a process that will identify both current and future human resources needs. What is this process called?
    A) organizational cost pressures and restructuring
    B) human capital competency
    C) human resources planning
    D) organizational effectiveness

120. What is the first step you should take when creating a human resources plan?
    A) formulate the action plan
    B) inventory current human resources
    C) analyze the organizational objectives
    D) run a return of investment for human resources costs

Bella is completing her degree in human resources and has an internship with a local organization. She is helping run some job analyses and creating job descriptions. Bella has been doing this since she learned about job descriptions as part of her college program.

121. Bella identifies that the person filling a particular role must hear well enough to communicate with other employees and also must be able to lift 20 pounds. These requirements will go into which part of a job description?
    A) general summary
    B) essential functions and duties
    C) disclaimer and approvals
    D) job specifications

122. Bella wants to include a statement that the job description is intended to outline the general duties and that other work can be assigned as needed. This type of statement would go into which part of a job description?
    A) general summary
    B) essential functions and duties
    C) disclaimer and approvals
    D) job specifications

Blaine has been tasked with improving the hiring process because the previous accounting manager had embezzled $10,000. The investigation revealed that the accounting manager had also embezzled at a previous employer. The organization realized its screening process needed to be improved to ensure that someone with this type of history was not hired in the future.

123. Blaine decides that he will talk to at least three individuals who have worked with the candidate in previous jobs. What is this type of screening called?
    A) background check
    B) reference check
    C) biographical check
    D) referral check

124. In performing a comprehensive background check, Blaine would NOT review which of the following?
    A) criminal records
    B) credit history
    C) professional certifications or licenses
    D) citizenship or work authorization

Aisha has just been promoted to training manager. Her organization, which employs approximately 200 people, is a food processor making jelly and jams. There is a significant requirement for employees to fully understand food safety measures to ensure the product is of the highest quality.

125. Aisha would like to conduct a training needs analysis for the company. She will be looking at three sources to analyze training needs. Which three sources should Aisha analyze?
    A) knowledge, skills, and attitude
    B) organization, job, and individual
    C) safety, quality, and production
    D) motivators, styles, and beliefs

126. Aisha knows it is important for learners to be ready to learn if the training program is going to be successful. Which of the following does NOT give Aisha an insight into the readiness of the learner?

A) ability to learn
B) learning style
C) motivation to learn
D) self-efficacy

The organization is interested in promoting from within and growing its workforce. This stems from a tight labor market as well as employee feedback that workers feel "stuck" in their roles. Hassan, the HR manager, has been tasked with implementing some programs to create internal movement for employees.

127. Hassan takes steps to assess employees' movement through opportunities over time. He is looking at employees'

A) career paths.
B) development plans.
C) performance appraisals.
D) assessment results.

128. Additionally, Hassan notes that most employees in the organization are between thirty and forty years old and have an average of eight to twelve years of experience. These individuals fall within which career stage?

A) early career
B) mid-career
C) late career
D) career end

Acme Manufacturing is a high-tech manufacturer of robotic parts. The company employs a number of engineers and IT personnel. The market Acme competes in is very competitive, and it is important that the organization is constantly introducing improved and innovative products. Jamal is the human resources manager who is putting in place programs that will support employees' continued creativity and learning.

129. Jamal wants to create a culture of lifelong learning and avoid initiatives that would discourage this atmosphere. Which initiative should Jamal discourage?

A) onsite anonymous feedback stations
B) mentorship programs for career planning
C) a more rigid disciplinary process
D) an internal e-learning platform for professional development

130. Jamal is looking at some creative ways for employees to feel refreshed and recharged. Which of the following might be a well-received program if cost is not a factor?

A) create goals and rewards for employees who complete certifications and degrees
B) develop a sabbatical program for employees
C) increase pay to reflect that most employees are working forty-five to fifty hours
D) move remote employees back into the office to encourage collaboration

An organization is falling behind in its competitiveness. It has been late on deliveries, significant errors in manufacturing and administration have occurred, and quality has been poor. The owners realize it is time to assess their personnel. They have hired Maria, a human resources consultant from an outsourcing firm, to review their team and processes.

131. One of the first items Maria suggests is implementing a program with a series of processes that identify employee performance measurements, communicate these measurements, and hold individuals accountable. What is this type of system called?

A) performance management
B) performance appraisal
C) performance-focused culture
D) job criteria

132. Maria helps the organization identify performance measurements. When looking at the accounting team, which measurements might she suggest as the MOST important?

   A) quantity of output
   B) presence at work
   C) timeliness of output
   D) cleanliness of work area

Ark Enterprises has a robust performance appraisal system. However, it seems as if the ratings are not consistent. The CEO has stated that he is tired of this system since it does not appear to give accurate information. However, as the HR manager, you know there is value in a good performance system and set off to determine what is wrong with the current process.

133. The first manager you meet with tells you that he does not believe anyone is exceptional and few are above average. Unless someone really goes the extra mile, in his opinion, everyone is average. What is this type of rating error called?

   A) recency effect
   B) similar-to-me effect
   C) central tendency
   D) varying standards

134. The second manager you meet with tells you he definitely has some star performers but also some poor performers. He tells you about Joe, who completes every task on time and is at work every day. However, Joe tends to be shy and does ot speak up in meetings. Therefore, the manager does not consider Joe to be a good performer. What type of rating error is this?

   A) halo effect
   B) horns effect
   C) central tendency
   D) sampling error

Answer Key

Knowledge-Based Questions

1. **C)** Before a merger deal is completed, HR should conduct a risk assessment to identify possible conflicts in order to proactively address any issues. HR processes and recognizing cultural differences should happen during the actual merger, while optimization of workforce typically happens after the merger.

2. **C)** As employees access processes or procedures, their perceived fairness of these is called procedural justice.

3. **A)** An adult learner usually has limited time and wants to know how the training will impact their work and improve productivity.

4. **D)** Internal consistency uses job analysis, wage data, and job descriptions to analyze the relative value and pay of a role as it relates to other roles in the organization.

5. **D)** The Consolidated Omnibus Budget Reconciliation Act (COBRA) provides continuation of group health care after loss of coverage due to reduction in hours, loss of employment, or other qualified reasons.

6. **C)** Situational questions can give insight into how a candidate handled a specific situation in the past and how they may handle it in the future.

7. **C)** An exit interview is conducted when an employee leaves an organization. The purpose of an exit interview is to gather information about why that person is leaving. This information may help the organization improve HR processes.

8. **C)** The relationship appears to be consensual, and the two parties are at the same level within the organization, which indicates it is most likely not a coerced relationship. However, since the relationship is impacting their performance, it is inadvisable and should be addressed.

9. **C)** Disparate impact happens when an employment policy has an adverse effect on a member of a protected class. In this case, women—who on average might be shorter and weigh less than the requirement—would be affected. There is no bona fide occupational qualification (BFOQ), since the manufacturer has not indicated that this type of restriction is needed for safe operation.

10. **B)** A job specification is a list of the knowledge, skills, and attributes (KSAs) required for a job. Job specifications are determined during the job analysis and are often included on the job description.

11. **D)** The similar-to-me effect happens when the rater allows characteristics they share with the employee to impact the rating.

12. **A)** The yield ratio is the ratio of applicants at one stage of hiring versus the number that moves on to the next stage.

13. **C)** A situational judgment test asks the candidate to make decisions or judgments about how they would handle certain situations.

14. **A)** This is bullying. Although Carl's behavior is unacceptable, this type of bullying is not considered illegal harassment because it is not focused on a specific protected class.

15. **B)** Arbitration uses a neutral third party to make a decision when there is an impasse.

16. **A)** When interviewing, it is best to focus on job-related questions. A hiring manager may need to know if a candidate graduated from high school. But the other questions could lead to an unlawful inquiry.

17. **B)** The NLRB does not restrict employers from talking about why they oppose the union or discussing the disadvantages. However, the employer cannot threaten or coerce employees.

18. **D)** Avoid using the term *permanent* regarding employment status in the offer letter, as this could imply an employment contract and become an issue if the employee is terminated in the future.

19. **B)** Job enrichment happens when more responsibilities are added within a specific role, increasing the depth of the role.

20. **C)** Organizational restructuring involves improving performance or productivity through analysis, elimination, and change of an organization's layers, head count numbers, and structure.

21. **B)** An environmental scan involves both an external and internal analysis of conditions that impact an organization. This information is often used during a strategic planning process.

22. **D)** During a talent surplus, employers must consider a number of options, including freezing hiring and limiting the number of hires, limiting the number of hours worked, reducing compensation, and introducing a voluntary separation program. All are designed to control labor costs.

23. **C)** Employees who do not meet certain exemption criteria are not exempted from the Fair Labor Standards Act. So even if they are paid on a salaried, or fixed, basis, these individuals must be paid time and a half for working 40+ hours in a workweek.

24. **A)** *BFOQ* stands for "bona fide occupational qualification." This is a legitimate work-related reason to exclude an otherwise protected class. In the case of the manufacturing company, an employee would have to be able to move and manage the product they are producing even though it may eliminate some candidates due to disability or age. Personality testing should not be used during the hiring process, and hiring only female servers in an Italian-themed restaurant is most likely illegal. Fall protection falls under OSHA regulations.

25. **A)** Title VII applies to all private employers with 15 or more employees.

26. **C)** An organization can achieve flexibility in staffing levels by using independent contractors during busy seasons or for specific projects. Additionally, it allows the organization to work with individuals who are subject-matter experts in certain areas.

27. **C)** Using an anonymous application system in which applicant names or other identifying information are hidden during initial screening will help focus selection on job-related criteria.

28. **A)** Flexible hours, compressed workweeks, and telecommuting are all ways that employers can support a work-life balance for their employees.

29. **D)** Jane is in a position of power over Deb, so it can never be assumed that Deb wants the relationship. Because Jane has offered Deb a raise in exchange for her companionship, this is more than inappropriate: it is quid pro quo, the exchange of a favor or benefit in return for something else.

30. **A)** Though the individual's disfigurement might cause others to be uncomfortable, this employee does not have physical or mental impairment that substantially limits a major life activity. Therefore, they are not disabled. However, due to others' assumptions or discomfort, this person may experience discrimination because there is a perceived disability.

31. **B)** Cost of recruiting is computed by dividing recruitment expenses by the number of hired.

32. **C)** The 1986 case of *Meritor Savings Bank vs. Vinson* was the first to show that the courts held that a hostile environment was discrimination under Title VII. It also established that *voluntary* does not mean *welcomed* when the initiator is in a position of authority.

33. **D)** Just because a function is included in a job description does not mean it is essential for the role.

34. **C)** Outplacement services provide support such as interviewing workshops or career counseling for displaced workers.

35. **C)** Though there is no evidence that negative employment decisions have been made due to Juan's heritage, the offensive comments and jokes are impacting Juan's workplace, creating an unhealthy environment that affects his performance and, therefore, employment.

36. **A)** Benchmarking is one approach used to assess HR effectiveness by comparing specific measures against those measures in other organizations.

37. **D)** People born between 1966 and 1980 are considered part of Generation X.

38. **B)** A psychological contract is the unwritten expectations that exist between an employee and the organization where they are employed.

39. **D)** Absenteeism describes an employee's failure to be at work during their scheduled time.

40. **B)** The Pregnancy Discrimination Act of 1978 requires that in companies employing fifteen or more employees, maternity leave be treated the same as other leaves, like medical or personal leave.

41. **A)** When measuring turnover costs, an employer may look at the cost of separation, replacement, and training along with other hidden costs such as employee morale, productivity impact, or customer satisfaction.

42. **B)** Title VII covers all private employers with fifteen or more employees who work twenty or more weeks in a year.

43. **B)** Under the ADA, employers are not required to provide devices or services to support an employee on a personal level beyond the workplace. A screen reader, however, might be necessary for an employee to do their job. The other devices are used outside of work for personal reasons.

44. **C)** Affirmative action plans compensate for historic discrimination against people in certain protected classes.

45. **C)** Title VII of the Civil Rights Act prohibits employment discrimination based on national origin. Having an Italian background refers to a person's national origin.

46. **D)** The Americans with Disabilities Act (ADA), passed in 1990, introduced the requirement of reasonable accommodation for persons with disabilities.

47. **C)** A sabbatical is a benefit in which employees are paid to leave work for job development or rejuvenation.

48. **C)** The recency effect occurs when the rater gives greater importance to recent events than to the overall performance.

49. **B)** The organization's culture is the shared values and beliefs that set norms and govern actions.

50. **D)** Retaliation occurs when an employer takes punitive action against an employee for an action, such as filing a claim.

51. **D)** *No fault* is a term typically used in an attendance or disciplinary policy. For instance, a no fault absence might not count toward a disciplinary process.

52. **C)** Though the hiring manager may have had good intentions, this question could reveal the candidate's age, which might lead to discrimination based on this protected characteristic.

53. **C)** Though the hiring manager may have had good intentions, this line of questioning could lead to information about religion and religious affiliation. It may also lead to information involving other protected information, such as familial status or national origin. During the interview process, it is best to avoid questions about religious holidays.

54. **D)** An economic strike happens when the two sides fail to reach an agreement during the collective bargaining process.

55. **A)** The *labor market* refers to the pool of individuals an organization attracts as applicants or employees.

56. **B)** State and local governments are not required to submit the EEO-1 report.

57. **A)** Job enlargement is the method of increasing the scope or span of a role by adding tasks or responsibilities.

58. **C)** Job rotation allows employees to move through a number of different roles to reduce boredom and stress of static work on the body.

59. **B)** Executive Orders 11246 and 11375 established the expectation that federal contractors and subcontractors would use affirmative action to reduce historic discrimination.

60. **C)** Negligent hiring is when an employer fails to perform a background check that might have revealed a potential issue, in this case, a violent employee with a criminal record.

61. **B)** Job specifications refer to the knowledge, skills, and abilities required to perform a role. A bachelor's degree in accounting falls into this category.

62. **C)** A performance standard uses tools such as job analysis or job description to set performance indicators and expectations for a specific role or job.

63. **C)** Before beginning a job analysis, it is important to identify the goal of the process and gain management support.

64. **B)** Using a questionnaire allows a large amount of job-related information to be collected quickly and cost-effectively.

65. **D)** A disclaimer section typically discusses change in duties, performing duties not listed, and employment relationship.

66. **B)** The job specifications should include the KSAs needed to perform the role in an acceptable manner.

67. **B)** The Office of Federal Contract Compliance Programs (OFCCP) is charged with ensuring that federal contractors and subcontractors are using nondiscriminatory practices.

68. **B)** The applicant pool is the total number of individuals who are actually being evaluated for selection.

69. **B)** A professional employer organization (PEO) supplies its own workforce to an employer.

70. **C)** The Equal Pay Act permits difference in pay if it is shown to be based on seniority, performance, or quality or quantity of work.

71. **C)** One of the most important steps an organization can take to ensure an intern's success is to spend time planning the organizational needs and creating meaningful work for the intern.

72. **D)** Employers should protect an employee's social security number and should not include it on any documents, such as an application, that might be shared or left in a public place. Many states have laws protecting employees' social security numbers.

73. **C)** Date of birth should not be included on the employee application because it could lead to age-related discrimination.

74. **B)** Preemployment tests must be both valid and reliable. This means they need to measure job-related skills and abilities and do so consistently between candidates. Validity relates to *what* the test is measuring, and reliability relates to consistency among applicants.

75. **A)** Performance management measures an individual's performance, coaches and develops employees, and rewards and recognizes performance.

76. **A)** An employee who is a citizen of one country but is working in another country is called an expatriate.

77. **C)** A "right to sue" letter is issued to the complainant if the employer rejects conciliation or the charge itself. The complainant then has ninety days to file a suit in federal court.

78. **B)** An employee who is not exempted, or nonexempt, from the Fair Labor Standards Act must be paid overtime.

79. **B)** This test might violate the Americans with Disabilities Act (ADA). Any test should be valid and reliable. In particular, a physical abilities test should be administered after the job offer and should focus on specific job-required measures to avoid disability discrimination.

80. **A)** Onboarding is the process of helping new hires integrate into their new work environment, learn their jobs, and transition into their roles.

Situational Judgment Questions

81. **A)** In this situation there might be unconscious biases that are influencing selection. The managers may be demonstrating the similar-to-me effect, a rating error. A signing bonus might get more applicants, but it does not solve the underlying problem. The employee referral program and the informal interview risk perpetuating the bias in selection. Creating a questionnaire based on true job needs may help coach the manager in making a decision based on skill rather than on other potentially discriminatory factors.

82. **C)** You should focus on the interviewing process itself and how to ensure that disparate treatment and disparate impact are not occurring. Other processes like the application system, the accommodation steps, and harassment guidelines are less relevant.

83. **B)** Benefits effectiveness calculates the return on investment of benefits. One way is to determine cost per employee. Other types of benefit effectiveness measurements include cost by employee group, cost as a percent of payroll, and benefit administrative costs.

84. **B)** The organization has forty employees and is not a sole proprietorship, so it must offer workers' compensation, unemployment, and social security. But it is not required under the Affordable Care Act to offer health insurance because it has fewer than fifty employees.

85. **C)** To be eligible for leave under the FMLA, an employee must have worked a minimum of twelve months and a minimum of 1,250 hours for the organization.

86. **C)** Visiting a cousin is not within the scope of the FMLA. FMLA leave may be used to care for a spouse, child, or parent with a serious health condition, not other family members.

87. **C)** For the employee to be paid through the workers' compensation system, his heart attack must have been caused through work. An analysis must be conducted to determine if the employee was doing anything job-related that could have triggered the heart attack, like shoveling or lifting a heavy part, or if it was caused by mitigating health issues.

88. **A)** The FMLA allows an organization to count workers' compensation leave toward the allotted twelve weeks. Depending on the severity of the employee's health condition, disability may be a concern, so the HR manager should be aware of any accommodations required under the ADA when the employee returns to work. Finally, according to OSHA, work-related injuries and illnesses must be reported.

89. **D)** Human resources can offer significant input into the strategic management process by offering analysis of workforce planning and design along with data obtained through human resources analytical assessments.

90. **C)** In outsourcing, a third-party provides specific services.

91. **D)** Job specifications refer to the KSAs needed to perform a job at a satisfactory level.

92. **C)** The major responsibilities and duties of a role are listed in the essential functions and duties section of the job description.

93. **C)** When an employee demonstrates problems with performance, the supervisor should raise these issues with the employee to give them a chance to improve. In this case, the supervisor should review Carla's mistakes with her and make a plan for improvement.

94. **B)** The Age Discrimination in Employment Act (ADEA) prohibits discrimination against workers aged forty and over. In Carla's case, though she is an older worker, she is not ready to retire. She has made some mistakes, but any concerns should be handled through coaching and focusing on the job-related issues, not on Carla's age.

95. **C)** The first step of a training process is to identify the training gaps in the workforce. Once Vicky has a clear understanding of what the training should focus on and what skills need to be improved, she can develop the learning objectives.

96. **A)** When developing learning objectives, trainers should consider items like the results of the needs assessment, content, materials, and learning styles. That way, clear training goals can be established.

97. **D)** Once the investigation has started, it is a good first step to meet with the accuser to fully understand the complaint, clarify details, and identify witnesses.

98. **C)** A hostile work environment is one in which a reasonable person would find certain behaviors offensive or abusive.

99. **B)** Flex time is a scheduling system that requires employees to work a specific number of "core hours" but permits approved variation in the schedule.

100. **A)** A compressed workweek is a scheduling system that allows workers to accomplish their work in fewer than five days per week.

101. **C)** The first step of a job analysis is to identify which roles or jobs to focus on. Then, select the method to obtain the most correct and valid data.

102. **C)** The observation method is used for jobs that include tasks that can be easily watched, like physical actions. This method is often used in an industrial setting and may include work sampling or a log.

103. **C)** The employee claims to have hearing loss and therefore most likely has a disability. This situation could involve discrimination and violation of the Americans with Disabilities Act (ADA).

104. **B)** A reasonable accommodation is a modification or adjustment to work that does not impose undue hardship on the organization. A headset that costs less than $100 would be considered a reasonable request.

105. **A)** The recruiting method involves choosing the medium to best advertise the available position.

106. **D)** The recruiting message is the way the organization explains the organization, the role, and its benefits to potential applicants.

107. **C)** Internal recruiting sources are methods of recruiting applicants that focus on resources inside the organization, like personnel, company databases, and company communication tools.

108. **D)** Employment agencies or headhunters are organizations that recruit and screen candidates to present to an organization. This is a contractual relationship that typically involves paying a certain percent of the first-year salary or an hourly rate to perform the recruitment work.

109. **B)** The Equal Employment Opportunity Commission (EEOC) requires private organizations with more than 100 employees to file an EEO-1 report that categorizes employees by race, ethnicity, gender, and job classification.

110. **A)** According to the US Department of Labor, a "federal subcontract" is an agreement or arrangement with a federal contractor for the furnishing of supplies or services or for the use of real or personal property, which is necessary to the performance of any one or more federal contracts. Federal subcontractors must have affirmative action plans.

111. **D)** To ensure adherence to child labor laws, it is legal to determine if an applicant is over the age of eighteen. All the other questions would reveal a protected class.

112. **C)** A birth certificate issued by a foreign government is not an acceptable document for verifying work eligibility in the United States.

113. **C)** The process of giving a candidate a thorough and accurate picture of the position is called a realistic job preview. The goal of this process is to reduce turnover by allowing the candidates to make an informed decision about the work.

114. **C)** A physical ability test is important in a job with high physical demands. However, the employer needs to be sure they are not violating the Americans with Disabilities Act (ADA) or the Age Discrimination in Employment Act (ADEA) by singling out individuals who fall within these protected classes. Additionally, this test must measure ability in job-related demands. By involving the occupational physician, Chris is introducing an objective evaluator. And, this evaluation is done post-offer to avoid violating provisions of the ADA.

115. **D)** The Americans with Disabilities Act (ADA) prohibits asking a candidate about past or current medical history. This includes workers' compensation history. Questions should pertain to the candidate's knowledge of and experience with safety.

116. **A)** Title VII of the Civil Rights Act prohibits discrimination based on religion. By asking which church candidates attend, the manager could be allowing religion to influence hiring decisions. She should simply ask if candidates are available to work on Sundays.

117. **B)** *TIPS* stands for "threats, interrogation, promises, and surveillance." The NLRB prohibits these behaviors during a union organization campaign.

118. **C)** Transferring or punishing a nurse is considered a threat and therefore would be in violation of the NLRA.

119. **C)** Human resources planning is the process of evaluating the human resources needs of an organization to identify a plan of action to support the overall company goals and objectives.

120. **C)** Understanding the goals and objectives of the organization is essential when creating a human resources plan. That way, human resources can better understand the demands on the human resources function in order to support the entire organization.

121. **D)** Physical requirements are part of the knowledge, skills, and abilities included in the job specifications.

122. **C)** Any legal disclaimers or approval signatures would be included in the disclaimer and approvals section of a job description.

123. **B)** A reference check is a process in which former coworkers of a candidate are interviewed about the candidate's previous performance and employment.

124. **D)** Citizenship and/or work authorization is verified post-offer when Form I-9 is completed to verify the identity and work authorization of an individual.

125. **B)** When conducting a training needs assessment, gaps and needs can be identified on an organizational, job, or individual basis. All levels of skills gaps and needs should be considered when designing a training program.

126. **B)** Learning style reflects *how* the learner learns rather than their readiness to learn. Ability to learn, motivation, and self-efficacy all relate to readiness to learn.

127. **A)** *Career path* refers to an employee's movement through the organization. This term can be applied to an individual or a role.

128. **B)** Employees between thirty and forty with eight to twelve years of experience are typically classified as mid-career. These people focus on career advancement, growth, and opportunity as they look to the next promotion.

129. **C)** Introducing a rigid disciplinary process while implementing a cultural change that supports employee learning and growth may send mixed messages. It may be more prudent to deal with individual issues one-on-one and later update the policy further if necessary.

130. **B)** Sabbaticals and paid vacations allow employees with high mental or physical demands to rejuvenate and refresh so that they can be more creative while at work.

131. **A)** Performance management is the system that measures performance, communicates it to employees and management, and holds individuals accountable for poor performance.

132. **C)** In accounting, it is important to have accurate work that is produced in a timely manner. That way, the business has the information needed to make decisions.

133. **C)** Central tendency errors occur when a manager gives most or all employees a rating that falls in the middle of the scale.

134. **B)** The horns effect happens when the rater allows one negative characteristic to influence the entire rating. In this case, Joe is a good performer who has one negative issue: he does not speak up during meetings. Instead of looking at the whole performance, the manager is focused on one negative issue.

www.triviumtestprep.com/shrm-online-resources

www.ingramcontent.com/pod-product-compliance
Lightning Source LLC
Chambersburg PA
CBHW080738300426
44114CB00019B/2621